REVOLUTIONARY LEADERSHIP

DR. KERRY MITCHELL BROWN

REVOLUTIONARY LEADERSHIP

A POWER PLAYBOOK FOR BLACK WOMEN

Entrepreneur | Books

Published by Entrepreneur® Books, Charleston, South Carolina.
An imprint of Advantage Media Group.

Printed in the United States of America.

10 9 8 7 6 5 4 3 2 1

ISBN: 979-8-89701-061-5 (Paperback)
ISBN: 979-8-89701-062-2 (eBook)

Library of Congress Control Number: 2026907072

Cover design by Lance Buckley.
Layout design by Megan Elger.

04-08-2026 2:10

To my daughters, Olivia Danté and Saige Lillian:
Here's to you claiming your power and realizing your promise.

CONTENTS

INTRODUCTION

The Imperative for Revolutionary Leadership

I have watched my daughters onstage, dancing and singing to their hearts' content, following the choreography and sheet music they know like the backs of their hands. I have watched every pirouette and listened to every high note with excitement and awe, not only at their skill and grace, but also at the joy they radiate as they command the stage. In those states, they show a freedom and fullness of life that I am always amazed and inspired by. I came to realize that, beyond their obvious talent, they inspired me because every effortlessly executed twist and twirl of their bodies and voices was a manifestation of the essence of their souls. This work required something deep within.

This was their soul-level work. And this book, *Revolutionary Leadership*, is my soul-level work.

The work I present to you is rooted in years of listening to Black women—in boardrooms and classrooms, church basements, and community rooms, on Zoom screens and in quiet moments after long workdays when the mask finally slips and the truth surfaces. It comes at a critical moment, as organizations and institutions continue to struggle with how to create environments that are genuinely inclusive and capable of meaningful transformation.

The numbers tell a part of this story. Although Black women make up nearly 8 percent of the US population, we hold just over 1 percent of top executive leadership roles.[1] In 2024, only two Black women, 0.4 percent of Black women executives, were serving as the CEOs of Fortune 500 companies. These figures do more than illustrate underrepresentation; they reveal the gap between public commitments to equity and the lived realities of those who are expected to carry the promise of progress.

We are also living in a time when both diversity and equity efforts are under attack and only superficially applied—too often symbolic rather than structural. What many organizations call "inclusion" remains uneven, conditional, or unstaffed. Through this book, I offer Black women leaders—and the organizations, teams, and communities they serve—evidence-based, equity-centered approaches for strengthening leadership, reshaping culture, and advancing human-centered transformation.

Long before this book took shape, I began studying, witnessing, and documenting the ways Black women lead—across workplaces, communities, and systems. My 2010 doctoral dissertation became one formal milestone in that journey, capturing research that affirmed what many Black women already knew in their bodies: Caregiving—for children, elders, partners, family, and community—is not separate from leadership.

For many Black women, caregiving develops the same skills demanded in formal leadership roles—coordination, decision-making under constraint, resource sharing, mediation, crisis navigation, account-

1 Joann S. Lublin, "Corporate Boards Diversify, but Leadership Lags," *USA Today*, March 16, 2023, https://www.usatoday.com/story/money/2023/03/16/corporate-america-diversity-lacking-senior-leadership/11464836002.

ability to others, and the maintenance of relationships and community sustainability. Care is not a side activity that happens outside of work. It is a leadership practice that shapes how responsibility is carried, how problems are solved, and how success is experienced, even when institutions fail to recognize or reward the labor required to sustain it.

Years later, in a world reshaped by COVID-19 and the racial justice uprisings of 2020, I returned to this research to understand how these conditions had transformed the realities of Black women's leadership. I gathered new data from Black women working inside organizations and from those leading as entrepreneurs—women navigating responsibility, visibility, and change across different professional landscapes. Across both groups, the pattern was unmistakable: Black women continue to lead, stabilize, organize, and hold others together, and still, the systems around us rarely share the cost of that labor.

This book grows out of that truth and out of a deep belief that Black women deserve pathways to leadership that do not require self-sacrifice as the cost of entry. It is designed to support Black women leaders as they build, transform, and thrive—and to guide organizations committed to becoming places of equity, learning, belonging, and repair. As the research makes clear, equitable and discrimination-free workplaces are not simply a moral imperative; they are essential to organizational integrity, innovation, and long-term success.[2]

As the research makes clear, equitable and discrimination-free workplaces are not simply a moral imperative; they are essential to organizational integrity, innovation, and long-term success.

2 Kerry Mitchell Brown, "Revolutionary Evidence: A 15+ Year Longitudinal Study of Black Women's Leadership, Visibility, and Thriving (2010–2025)," unpublished manuscript.

Though the figures presented earlier appear bleak, we are at a pivotal moment for multiple reasons. Historical leadership innovations are finally being recognized, particularly through lived experiences and changes in the world's demographics. Traditional leadership models are being questioned now that the limitations of these frameworks are glaringly obvious and the workplace is ready for effective alternatives. This shift is ushering this revolutionary leadership into the mainstream and creating the conditions for Black women, their workplaces, and their communities to fully live out the benefits of this once "radical" approach, which prioritizes authenticity, community connection, and collective well-being.

Revolutionary Leadership is designed to support current and aspiring Black women leaders, progressive organizations, strategic leadership development initiatives, and system-wide transformation. By the end of the book, you will understand how to move closer to your promise, leveraging new strategies while overcoming the many barriers you might encounter along the way. You will have workable solutions, real-world scenarios, and proven approaches for creating the changes you need. Whether or not you lead teams, you will be able to operate with clarity, confidence, and purpose.

As a Black scholar-practitioner and a woman with a PhD in organizations and management and over thirty years of dedicated industry success and independent research, I am well-equipped to help you champion your own revolutionary leadership. I have worked with over fifty organizations and more than 250 partners worldwide, transforming the lives of over 500 leaders, and I have inspired over 3.7 million participants through over five hundred workshops. Through my consultancy, kmb, I have worked with Fortune 100 companies, nonprofits, and government institutions, gathering insights that are relevant to the context, regardless of how unique it may be. My lived experience navigating white male–dominated workplaces while raising two sets of children more than two decades apart means I've been the only Black woman in the room more times than I can count. I've made all the mistakes (some of which I will share with you in this book), but through those, I've found solutions that you can use.

Revolutionary Leadership doesn't just offer individual navigation strategies or organizational change frameworks. It provides an integrated approach that addresses both simultaneously, creating possibilities for transformation at every level. The book is organized into four parts.

In part 1, Understanding the Landscape, we look at why Black women had to develop revolutionary leadership approaches in the first place. You'll gain insight into the historical context and understand the systems that made innovation necessary. It's not just complaining about barriers. It's showing how those barriers created opportunities for breakthrough thinking.

In part 2, Strategic Power, you'll find research-backed strategies for building influence. This isn't the traditional advice that doesn't work for us. Instead, I provide approaches to relationship building, visibility, and resource management that have been proven to drive Black women's advancement and success.

Part 3, Transforming Cultures, moves beyond the individual to focus on entire organizations and systems. With frameworks for measuring real change, not just surface improvements, you'll learn how to go from surviving systems to redesigning them.

Part 4, Legacy and Liberation, is about sustainability and passing knowledge forward. How do you build lasting power? How do you create pathways for the next generation? And how do you do this work without burning out?

Filled with research findings, assessment frameworks, and action steps, each part provides tools readers can use immediately to create change.

I began by revealing that *Revolutionary Leadership* is my soul work. What I didn't mention was why. When I was in my doctoral program, almost twenty years ago, researching what worked for Black women's career mobility and success while living it, I was raising two kids as a divorced single mother. I remember sitting in leadership meetings where colleagues debated theories about barriers facing women of color, which didn't always mean Black women, and it was always in comparison to others. Yet there I was, the actual subject of their research, struggling with childcare during my comprehensive exams. The disconnect was obvious. That experience taught me that lived experience and research must work together. For years, I wished the wisdom and insights bound in this book existed so that women like me would not have to go through these struggles unaided. Now, they don't.

I am grateful you've chosen to read this book. I hope the insights and experiences I share here offer you the lessons and confidence you need to lead differently. Not only that, but I hope the book activates within you the transformative power you already possess.

It is historically proven that we do not just survive systems; we transform them. And that transformation always begins with the audacity to dream beyond what others think is possible for someone who looks like us, sounds like us, and carries the wisdom of communities like ours.

Are you ready to realize the fullness of your revolutionary leadership?

Let's go.

PART 1

Understanding the Landscape

CHAPTER 1
The Revolutionary Pathmaker

I am deliberate
and afraid
of nothing.
AUDRE LORDE

You know her when you see her. It goes beyond her looks. It's about her presence when she steps into the room. Quiet or flamboyant, colorful or subtle, whatever her personality and aesthetic, there is something about her that makes you pay attention. Is it how she carries herself? Is it what she has to say or how she says it? Perhaps it is her indomitable spirit and her fortitude of character? Whatever it is, you know she holds a power that not everyone has. In this opening chapter, we take a close look at the type of leader who embodies revolutionary leadership. We call her the *Revolutionary Pathmaker*. Here, we will come to understand what makes one a Revolutionary Pathmaker and explore the historical relevance of their innovative leadership approaches. We will also discuss evidence-based insights, decades of research, and data that informed the findings of this book. But, first things first …

What Is a Revolutionary Pathmaker?

A Revolutionary Pathmaker is a Black woman who creates routes where none exist. She doesn't just navigate broken systems; she builds new ways through them. Her approaches are revolutionary because they challenge how success is achieved. She is a pathmaker because she creates routes for others.

History offers bountiful examples of these Revolutionary Pathmakers: Harriet Tubman, abolitionist and civil rights icon; Rosa Parks, trailblazing activist; Angela Davis, scholar and public intellectual; Shirley Chisholm, former congresswoman; Madam C. J. Walker, business pioneer; Maya Angelou, literary genius; Audre Lorde, sensational writer; Toni Morrison, Nobel laureate; Dorothy Hebborn, Miriam Makeba, Winnie Madikizela-Mandela, and Ella Baker, civil rights leaders; and Ellen Johnson Sirleaf, former president of Liberia. All are legendary beacons of such leadership. More contemporary examples include screenwriter and producer Shonda Rhimes, musician Angélique Kidjo, tennis champion Serena Williams, Pan-African leader Arikana Chihombori-Quao, Zimbabwean activist Glanis Changachirere, writer and producer Issa Rae, Nigerian business tycoons Damilola Odufuwa and Odunayo Eweniyi, former NASA astronaut Dr. Mae Jemison, filmmaker and screenwriter Ava DuVernay, lawyer and politician Stacey Abrams, poet Amanda Gorman, former Vice President Kamala Harris, and Senators Angela Alsobrooks of Maryland and Lisa Blunt Rochester of Delaware. There are many other Revolutionary Pathmakers leading change in our local communities, women whose names you and I may never have heard. Here's a story of such a champion.

THE BREAKFAST CLUB

You have to act as if it were possible to radically transform the world. And you have to do it all the time.
ANGELA DAVIS

A few years ago, I worked with a Black woman who was the only person of color on her company's leadership team. Traditional networking wasn't working for her. She couldn't golf with the guys or join their after-work drinks. As a leader, she knew the importance of networking and how the lack of it would impede her success. So she created something different—something that not only helped her network but added value for the others who joined. She started hosting monthly breakfasts for women across all departments. These breakfast meetings were not just for executives. Administrative assistants, project managers, analysts—everyone was welcome.

Other leaders thought she was wasting time on people who couldn't help her career. They could not fathom that, among the cups of hot coffee and plates of toast, hash browns, bacon, eggs, and sometimes grits, she could be building something of value. They could not conceive of this consistent and voluntary social engagement generating anything that could translate into bankable value. But value is exactly what came out of it—especially cross-functional knowledge and a network that got things done. The biggest indisputable evidence of how impactful these meetings were was that this woman was promoted to the role of vice president two years after she launched these breakfast meetups. Her breakfast network became the unofficial communication system that made the whole company run better.

My research shows this pattern everywhere: Black women gain from organizing communities and building coalitions, and then they apply them to transform entire systems.[3 4]

POWER ACTIVATION PROMPT

Consider the host of exemplary leaders we named in this chapter, as well as at least one Black woman you know in your own life. What do you recognize as the actions of a Revolutionary Pathmaker?

Do you count yourself as a revolutionary leader in your community? Why, or why not?

The Revolutionary Pathmaker's approach is unique because she figured out how to turn community organizing into corporate leadership. She learned how to use her church committee experience to run board meetings. Somehow, she realized she could adapt the relationship-building skills used at home for her professional networks. Women who learned to navigate complex community dynamics became experts at organizational politics. Women who managed volunteer board budgets with no resources became financial strategists. These

3 Kerry Mitchell Jones, "A Quantitative Study Examining the Impact of Personal Relationships in the Professional Lives of Black Women" (PhD diss., Capella University, 2010).

4 Kerry Mitchell Brown, "Revolutionary Evidence: A 15+ Year Longitudinal Study of Black Women's Leadership, Visibility, and Thriving (2010–2025)," unpublished manuscript.

aren't famous names that you would recognize. They are women who are creating new approaches every day, in companies, nonprofits, and government agencies, often without realizing how revolutionary their methods are. That's part of why I wrote this book. To document these approaches and show how they can be replicated.

When traditional leadership strategies fail, revolutionary leadership often excels. When hierarchy becomes a barrier, these trailblazing women learn to build influence through relationships.

Historical Context

Let's consider the Revolutionary Pathmakers of previous eras, such as Harriet Tubman, Rosa Parks, and Shirley Chisholm. What you may notice about these women is that their leadership roles were rational and necessary; they were imperative to the vibrancy and even the survival of the collective in the community.

The reality is that Black women have been creating pathways in hostile spaces since we got here. We didn't have a choice. During enslavement, when Black women were, by definition, systematically excluded from formal power structures, we organized underground networks to protect children and plan escapes. We learned to build influence without authority because we had no legal standing.

After emancipation, segregation kept us out of white institutions. So, when no one would educate Black children, we built schools. When banks wouldn't serve Black communities, we created mutual aid societies. We established organizations that championed our causes, ensuring we advocated for ourselves and future generations. We had to innovate because we were locked out of existing systems.

In the 1960s, while everyone talked about male civil rights leaders, Black women were doing the organizing that made the movement work. We planned the bus boycotts, registered voters, and washed the dishes. We kept organizations running.

We weren't just surviving. We were innovating. We developed leadership approaches that the business world is finally catching up to, even if it won't acknowledge it. Community-centered decision-making. Relationship-based influence. Collective problem-solving. These aren't new leadership trends. Black women have been using these approaches for generations.

White men built leadership systems based on their experiences. Golf courses, old boys' networks, and mentorship that happened over drinks. These weren't designed for us. We weren't allowed in.

Add gender to race, and the complexity exponentially compounds. We face different stereotypes from Black men, different expectations from white women. In addition, the residual impact of enslavement that persists to this day further differentiates the experiences of Black women from those of their white counterparts.

Even when legislation in the 1960s "removed" the barriers in the US, the informal systems and practices stayed the same. You still needed sponsors who looked like you and understood your experience. You still needed to fit cultural norms that weren't built for Black women.

Globally, colonialism created similar patterns. European powers imposed racial hierarchies that put Black women at the bottom. Whether in the Caribbean, Africa, or elsewhere, we learned to work around traditional power structures and systems designed to exclude us.

We learned to build power without formal authority because we rarely had formal authority. We learned to create change from the margins because that's where we were forced to work. What looked like innovation to everyone else was a necessity for us. We've always been Revolutionary Pathmakers because we had to be.

Revolutionary Pathmakers diligently innovated and used the networks they had access to: churches, sororities, community organizations, and even extended family systems. They learned to build influence from informal authority because formal authority was rarely available to them. They developed relationship-based leadership because they couldn't rely on positional power. They learned collective decision-making because they had to get buy-in from people who didn't report to them.

The irony is that the very systems that excluded us forced us to get creative. What looked like disadvantages became sources of innovation. We built new approaches that work better in complex, diverse organizations. Unfortunately, with this exposition, everyone finally started paying attention, and the attacks and systemic barriers intensified.

Research Insights

My work on Black women's leadership did not begin in academic study—it emerged through years of professional practice, observation, and dialogue with Black women who were leading across organizations, communities, and systems. My 2010 doctoral dissertation[5] became a formal documentation of that ongoing inquiry, capturing patterns that had long been present in our lived experiences.

That earlier research revealed something deeply resonant: Caregiving—for children, elders, partners, family, and community—is not separate from how Black women lead. Care shapes identity, purpose, and meaning. It is woven into our leadership, our sense of responsibility, and how success is understood. The same behaviors that sustain caregiving—anticipating needs, coordinating resources, supporting others through transition, and ensuring stability during periods of

5 Jones, "Quantitative Study."

stress—often mirror the invisible labor required to keep teams and organizations functioning.

Yet even then, the findings reflected a tension many Black women recognize intuitively: Although caregiving-aligned leadership behaviors often benefit workplaces, they do not consistently translate into institutional reward or upward mobility. Instead, they are frequently treated as expected, natural, or informal contributions rather than recognized as strategic labor that creates value.

Fifteen years later, in a world transformed by COVID-19 and racial justice uprising, I returned to this work to reexamine these dynamics. I found they had evolved and, in many cases, intensified.[6] Studying Black women's experiences within organizations and as entrepreneurs side by side allowed me to see more clearly how caregiving, visibility, networking, and institutional context shape opportunity, advancement, and sustainability across different environments.

This research is not simply descriptive—it is a lens through which we understand power, responsibility, and the conditions under which Black women are expected to lead.

Building on the foundational 2010 research,[7] my 2025 analysis[8] examines how these forces operate in the present moment and what they reveal about leadership, sustainability, and systemic constraint. This research does not simply document outcomes; it illuminates the conditions under which Black women are expected to lead, adapt, and persist across inequitable systems.

---

6 Brown, "Revolutionary Evidence."

7 Ibid.

8 Ibid.

Revolutionary Leadership Model

From this body of research, a leadership framework emerged that I call the *Revolutionary Leadership Model.* Rather than prescribing a set of individual strategies, this model reflects the historically grounded, community-anchored, and resilience-producing approaches that Black women have developed and refined across generations in response to structural constraints and cultural expectations.

Integrating historical leadership traditions with contemporary realities, the model highlights practices that enable Black women to navigate complexity, build power, and sustain meaning in environments that are not always designed to support them. These practices include innovation and creative problem-solving; resisting assimilation that demands self-erasure; and cultivating networks of connection, care, and solidarity—what I call *friend raising*—as both a leadership practice and a form of collective preservation.

INNOVATION

Innovation refers to new approaches for achieving goals, career mobility, and sustainability. Consensus building is one such innovative approach by Revolutionary Pathmakers. Black women learned to build consensus by managing extended families, church committees, cookouts, and other such community engagements. We had to get everyone on board because we couldn't just give orders and expect compliance.

For decades, corporate America called this type of leadership inefficient. Now people call it *inclusive leadership* and pay consultants millions to teach it.

Another innovative approach championed by Black women is community care. Black women have always understood that taking care of people is not separate from getting results. Rather, it's how you get sustainable results. Business schools are just figuring this out.

These approaches are transformative now because traditional leadership is failing. Command-and-control techniques don't work in complex, diverse organizations. Critics of the Revolutionary Leadership Model may argue that this model is not revolutionary, but I argue that what makes this model revolutionary is not that it applies to something completely new—it's that *it actually works.* While everyone else was stuck on what looked powerful and authoritative but was also dehumanizing, patronizing, individualistic, and cruel, Revolutionary Pathmakers realized that effective leadership could be humane, collaborative, respectful, and filled with compassion for others.

NONCONFORMITY

Conformist approaches tell Black women to fit into existing systems. Speak softer. Network like everyone else. Don't be too direct. Follow the traditional career ladder. Be grateful. If they were to state the quiet part out loud, these approaches would say, "Just be palatable to white male leadership standards."

On the other hand, revolutionary approaches say the system is the problem, not you. Instead of changing yourself to fit broken systems, create new ways to succeed.

Conformist networking says join the golf club, go to happy hour, build relationships with senior white men (or people who act like them). Revolutionary networking leverages the relationships you already have. Use your church connections. Your sorority network. Your community ties.

Conformist thinking says this is unprofessional. Revolutionary thinking says this is strategic. When it comes to visibility, for example, conformist approaches tell you to speak up in meetings, but not too much—you wouldn't want to appear threatening. Revolutionary approaches say to create your own platforms. Host your own meetings. Build your own influence networks. Launch your own community-building campaigns.

Revolutionary networking leverages the relationships you already have. Use your church connections. Your sorority network. Your community ties.

The conformist approach assumes the existing system will eventually include you if you play by the rules. Revolutionary approaches assume the system needs changing and that you're the one to do it.

My research shows that revolutionary approaches work better than conformist ones. However, to be successful with revolutionary approaches requires that you stop trying to be what other people think a leader should be.[9]

FRIEND RAISING

Community building, capacity building, or what I like to call friend raising is another pillar of revolutionary leadership. My research shows that Black women who actively participate in church and community activities report significantly higher career satisfaction and stronger professional networks than those who don't.[10] [11] What makes this revolutionary? These connections aren't just about advancing careers. They're about building power structures that look different from traditional professional networking.

9 Ibid.

10 Jones, "Quantitative Study."

11 Brown, "Revolutionary Evidence."

The relationships we build in our communities aren't separate from our professional lives. They're a training ground for leadership skills that translate directly into workplace success.

The research is clear: Friend raising isn't a distraction from professional development. It's a form of professional development that honors who we are while building the capacity we need to lead effectively. The women in my studies who maintained strong community ties reported better work–life integration, more authentic leadership styles, and greater resilience during career challenges.[12] [13] They weren't choosing between community and career. They were leveraging one to strengthen the other.

What the Research Reveals

My 2025 study[14] deepens our understanding of how Black women navigate leadership across both organizational and entrepreneurial contexts. Rather than pointing to individual strategies as the primary drivers of advancement, my findings highlight how promotion, opportunity, growth, and well-being are shaped by structural conditions—including caregiving responsibilities, visibility, crisis exposure, and the relational labor Black women are required to carry.

In organizational roles, internal visibility—such as leading initiatives, taking on high-exposure assignments, and engaging with senior decision-makers—has been associated with higher promotion trajectories over time. Yet, visibility does not always correspond with a stronger sense of opportunity, support, or protection. For many women, visibility makes inequality more perceptible, even as they advance.

---

12 Ibid.

13 Ibid.

14 Ibid.

Caregiving emerged as an especially consequential factor. Black women carrying heavier caregiving responsibilities were less likely to experience upward mobility in organizational settings and reported lower business growth and satisfaction as entrepreneurs, particularly in the years following COVID-19. Care remains deeply meaningful—but the systems surrounding Black women do not consistently share the cost of that labor.

Networking also shifted in meaning. Rather than serving primarily as a pathway to advantage, increased networking activity—especially among entrepreneurs—was often reflective of stabilization and recovery work in response to instability. The women who networked most intensely were frequently working to keep their careers, clients, and businesses afloat, not simply expanding their influence.

Across both pathways, many Black women described a reframing of success. Instead of defining success only through title ascension or business expansion, women increasingly emphasized sustainability, autonomy, well-being, and the ability to care for themselves and those they supported without erasure or exhaustion.

This is not a story of individual inadequacy. The findings reveal systems that continue to rely on Black women's competence, resilience, and leadership—while too rarely redistributing the weight of responsibility, care, and emotional labor. They also affirm the necessity of environments that not only benefit from Black women's leadership but also sustain it.

Before we conclude, let me share with you my story of what led me to become a Revolutionary Pathmaker.

SCRATCH THOSE UNWRITTEN RULES

If they don't give you a seat at the table, bring a folding chair.
SHIRLEY CHISHOLM

I learned early that the traditional career path wasn't for someone like me. I was a young Black mother trying to build a career in finance. A long day at work was often followed by an evening of bath time, dinnertime spent enticing my children to eat their greens, and repeated prompts to brush their teeth and go to bed. The networking happened at times I couldn't attend. The unwritten rules weren't explained to people who looked like me.

So, I started building my own approach. I used relationships from outside work, such as community organizations. I turned my caregiving experience into management skills. I stopped trying to fit into their boxes and started creating my own. The liberation that came with shedding these societal pressures was priceless.

Later, to be eligible for a promotion and a higher salary, I went back to school for my MBA. I didn't stop there, going on to earn a PhD, all while raising kids. Everyone thought I was crazy. They said it was too complicated, that I had too many responsibilities. But I knew I needed the research to back up what I was seeing in the workplace.

When I left the workforce to start my consultancy, people said I was throwing away security. But I'd learned that security for Black women often means staying small. I wanted to create something bigger.

Raising two sets of children decades apart taught me something important. The barriers I faced in the nineties are different from those I face as a working mom now. But the underlying patterns are the same. Black women must still create our own pathways.

That's why I've updated my research. The workplace has changed, but we're still innovating around exclusion. We're still being Revolutionary Pathmakers because we must be.

KEY TAKEAWAYS

- Revolutionary Pathmakers create new routes instead of following existing ones that don't work for them.
- Black women have always been pathmakers out of necessity, developing innovative approaches when traditional leadership has failed.
- Community-based skills translate directly into professional power when applied strategically.
- What others call unconventional, pathmakers call strategic adaptations to broken systems.
- Revolutionary approaches work better in today's complex organizations than traditional command-and-control methods.

ACTION STEPS

- Map your community networks: List the relationships and connections from your church, family, volunteer work, and neighborhood that could become professional assets.

- Identify one traditional workplace rule that doesn't fit your situation. Brainstorm a few alternative approaches that might get you the same result.
- Find your pathmaker examples: Look for Black women in your industry, organization, or network, and study their approaches. Note their steps and identify what you can emulate in your own journey.
- Start one relationship-building activity this week that uses your existing networks instead of traditional professional networking.
- Practice translating your community skills. Take one skill you use at home or in your volunteer work and apply it to a current workplace challenge.

CHAPTER 2
Transforming Exclusionary Systems

When my brothers try to draw a circle to exclude me,
I shall draw a larger circle to include them.
PAULI MURRAY

No matter who you are, you've experienced it. A roadblock, a temporary or seemingly permanent impediment to your advancement in some area of your life. In this chapter, we will explore the concept of *exclusionary systems* and how you can transform them. As might be clear from the name, the goal of such systems is not inclusion, but exclusion. These systems ensure that groups of people do not benefit equally. In the workforce, exclusionary systems can be inconvenient at best and a career killer at worst.

Exclusionary systems do not always look obvious. They are often hidden in everyday business operating practices and normalized or contemporary means of accomplishing outcomes. And they favor people who already have access, privilege, and power. Because of how valuable these systems are to beneficiaries, the systems maintain themselves. There is no need for any individual or group to actively and blatantly discriminate—it happens simply through the way business is done and organizational culture operates.

Exclusionary systems affect everyone differently. For those who are historically excluded, the effects of these systems are not only perpetual but also cumulative. Take white women, for instance. While white women experience privilege because of their race, they face their own limitations because of the gendered systemic barriers they must navigate. Conversely, Black men can leverage certain privileges at work and in the world because of their gender, but these are limited by their race. Black women, on the other hand, experience exclusionary systems from the intersection of their race and their gender. As such, the negative impact of these systems on their career trajectory is exponential.

CASE STUDY: FROM DEPORTEE TO LEGEND—CLAUDIA JONES

You may not control all the events that happen to you, but you can decide not to be reduced by them.

MAYA ANGELOU

Imagine everything you know and love suddenly being snatched away from you. That was the circumstance Claudia Jones found herself in when she was deported from the USA in 1995.[15] *Born Claudia Vera Cumberbatch in Trinidad and Tobago in 1915, during her childhood, her family migrated to New York City in*

15 "Claudia Jones Research Collection: 1935–1998," New York Public Library Archives and Manuscripts, accessed January 2026, https://archives.nypl.org/scm/21209.

> *search of a better life. For the next forty years, Claudia developed herself into a journalist, activist, and political changemaker.*[16]
>
> *Over the years, she helped organize rallies that put a spotlight on egregious injustices toward the Black community, such as that of the famous Scottsboro case in which nine young Black men were wrongfully charged with the rape of two white women.*[17]
>
> *As a result of her advocacy work, Claudia, who had not yet become a US citizen, was deported to England, where she settled in London.*[18] *Using her exceptional writing and editing skills, management experience, and intellect, she took over the* West Indian Gazette, *then a humble publication that disseminated Black news from London and around the world. The success of this publication helped her launch the Caribbean Carnival, which still runs to this day and is now known as the Notting Hill Carnival.*[19]

Claudia's story shows how exclusionary systems work. She spent forty years fighting for justice in America. The system's response? Deportation. When her activism threatened the status quo, they didn't just ignore her; they removed her.

But Claudia didn't stop. She went to London and built new platforms. She revived a struggling publication and created a community event that still runs today. The system tried to erase her.

16 Joan Hibler, "Claudia Jones," in *Encyclopedia Britannica*, last modified December 21, 2025, https://www.britannica.com/biography/Claudia-Jones.

17 Ibid.

18 Ibid.

19 Clarissa Atkinson, "Claudia Jones: Brief Life of an Intersectional Activist: 1915–1964," *Harvard Magazine*, August 6, 2020, https://www.harvardmagazine.com/2020/08/features-vita-claudia-jones.

She became a legend instead. That's what working against exclusionary systems looks like. You build anyway.

POWER ACTIVATION PROMPT

Think about a workplace rule, process, or tradition that consistently works against you or people like you. How would you redesign that system if you had the authority?

Research Insights

Studies show that Black women with more family responsibilities are more likely to get promoted than those with fewer obligations. This finding contradicts the traditional career advice often extolled as an immutable truth that Black women cannot have a thriving career, a happy family, and a healthy private life.[20] Traditional wisdom purports that family responsibilities hold women back. These findings fly in the face of the demand placed on Black women to choose between their career advancement and caregiving responsibilities.

Black women juggling children, aging parents, and household management are developing skills their childless colleagues don't have. They are learning to manage complex schedules, build consensus among different personalities, and get results with limited resources.

More importantly, Black women have stopped trying to succeed in systems that penalize them for having responsibilities. They create new approaches that work with their lives instead of against them. Instead of the norm, they network through school events, volunteer activities, and church and community committees. They build influence by solving problems others can't handle. They demonstrate

20 Jones, "Quantitative Study."

leadership by managing complexities that make executive challenges look simple.

The organizations that recognized this promoted these Black women. The ones that stuck to traditional thinking lost them to their competitors. Black women don't succeed despite systemic barriers. We succeed by transforming the systems themselves.

Black women don't succeed despite systemic barriers. We succeed by transforming the systems themselves.

Structures that Suppress Innovative Leadership

Exclusionary systems don't just keep Black women out. They also crush the innovative leadership approaches Black women bring when they do get in. You can see this pattern everywhere. A Black woman gets hired or promoted. She brings fresh ideas based on her community-organizing experience. She suggests collaborative decision-making models. She proposes ways to solve problems that no one else has thought of.

And then the organizational structures kick in, but not with obvious rejection. Instead, it's something more subtle. The very design of how work gets done makes it nearly impossible for the Black woman's approach to take root.

This is where exclusion shifts from blocking entry to blocking impact. Black women are in the building now. But the building wasn't designed for how they lead.

Four main structures do most of the damage: military-style hierarchies, network exclusions, performance review traps, and innovation penalties. Each one targets a different aspect of how Black women lead. Together, they form a system that suppresses the exact innovations organizations claim they want.

Let's look at how each one works.

MILITARY-STYLE HIERARCHIES

Walk into most organizations, and you'll see the same power structure. Decisions come from the top. Everyone else follows orders. It is corporate life modeled on the military.

This setup creates a particular problem for Black women. When good ideas only count if they come from the C-suite, and Black women are rarely in the C-suite, their insights get lost. Black women see inefficiencies. They spot opportunities. They understand customer needs that leadership misses. But the rigid chain of command means their knowledge stays trapped at the lower levels.

The military model assumes the people at the top know best. But those leaders often lack the ground-level view that Black women have. They don't see what's happening with frontline customers. They miss the daily friction that slows down teams. They can't spot the talent being wasted because someone doesn't fit the traditional leadership mold.

When a Black woman in middle management identifies a better process, she must push it up through layers of approval. Each layer adds delay. Each person in the chain can kill the idea. By the time it reaches decision-makers, the moment has passed, or the proposal has been watered down beyond recognition.

This isn't just about Black women losing credit for their ideas. The whole organization suffers. Companies pay for diverse perspectives and then build structures that silence them.

NETWORK EXCLUSION

High-level strategic jobs are frequently filled through internal networks and personal connections, not through job postings or formal processes. This means that deserving individuals who lack the necessary connections are often not considered for these positions.

Black women have limited access to internal networks because the informal spaces where power gets shared happen outside the office. Golf outings. Dinner parties. Happy hours that run late. Weekend conferences. These settings favor people who share similar backgrounds and life circumstances. Executives groom people who feel familiar.

This happens by design. Organizations want diverse leadership, but they build advancement processes that require extensive after-hours networking. They reward frequent travel for relationship building. They value "culture fit" without examining whose culture sets the standard. Sponsorship stays informal, following along existing social lines.

Black women not in these networks don't get considered for strategic roles. Without strategic roles, they can't access the networks. The loop reinforces itself.

Qualified Black women almost never attain high-level strategic leadership roles this way. Not from lack of capability. From systematic denial of access.

PERFORMANCE REVIEW TRAP

Traditional performance reviews punish nontraditional leadership styles. In many traditional work environments, attention and recognition are afforded to those who are the loudest in the room, regardless of whether they are the most competent or deserving. Performance reviews also reward people who promote themselves and fit into existing molds, but these are not typical characteristics of Black women leaders. Revolutionary Pathmakers tend to work in silence, stealthily attaining their goals.

INNOVATION PENALTIES

When Black women bring forward new ideas or challenge the status quo, they often face consequences instead of recognition. This is the innovation penalty.

Fortunately, there is extensive data on the correlation between innovation and companies with diverse teams or teams led by Black women. The results are clear: Diverse teams generate more money, capture new markets, and manage change more efficiently.[21]

How Exclusion Creates Innovation

Systemic barriers that are recreated inside organizations force Black women to adapt, innovate, and become resilient to survive. This has paradoxically created conditions in which Black women can thrive and succeed. Unfortunately, this success against the odds is often met with backlash and barriers that undermine our progress. But Black women continue to turn these conditions into fuel for further adaptation, innovation, and resilience. Let's consider a couple of examples of how exclusion has created innovation.

21 Vivian Hunt et al., "Diversity Matters Even More: The Case for Holistic Impact," McKinsey & Company, December 5, 2023, https://www.mckinsey.com/featured-insights/diversity-and-inclusion/diversity-matters-even-more-the-case-for-holistic-impact.

MEETING EXCLUSION

When Black women are unable to access informal decision-making conversations, on golf courses and in bars, they create cross-functional breakfast meetings and working lunches. These alternative meeting opportunities become more inclusive and productive because of their focus on work outcomes rather than social compatibility, as is the case for traditional networking.

MENTORSHIP GAP

Many senior leaders won't prioritize mentorship for Black women, so Black women are often left out of traditional mentorship relationships. In response, Black women have developed group mentoring circles and peer coaching networks. Research shows these collective approaches are more effective than one-on-one mentoring because they provide multiple perspectives and avoid dependency on a single relationship.[22]

FUNDING CONSTRAINTS

When banks elected not to fund Black women entrepreneurs, Black women created community-based lending circles and crowdfunding approaches. These models, which build stronger community support and reduce financial risk through diversified backing, are now used in several industries and across the Black diaspora. Though Black women remain underserved in the financial inclusion space, data shows that, regardless of income bracket, Black women around the world are

22 Brown, "Revolutionary Evidence."

typically good savers. They are also exceptional at investing back into their families and so improving their lives.[23]

VISIBILITY BARRIER

When Black women were excluded from high-profile assignments, they started creating their own platforms through internal presentations, cross-departmental projects, and external speaking opportunities. This *outside-in* approach to building credibility is now recognized as more sustainable than waiting for internal recognition. We will delve deeper into the outside-in approach in subsequent chapters.

NETWORK ACCESS

Elite professional associations are naturally exclusive. For Black women, accessing these associations is almost impossible. Locked out, Black women have leveraged church networks, sorority connections, and community organizations for business relationships. These values-based networks have proved more loyal and trustworthy than transactional professional relationships.

Examples of Black Women Transforming Barriers

The examples are endless. Africa's "Iron Lady," Her Excellency Ellen Johnson Sirleaf of Liberia, is a prime example. She led the way as Africa's first democratically elected female president, all the while furthering the empowerment of women. In 2011, she attained a Nobel Peace Prize alongside Leymah Gbowee (an activist) and Tawakkol

23 Nomsa Daniels, "Women's Financial Inclusion in Africa: Barriers, Costs and Opportunities," Open Society Initiative for Southern Africa, December 1, 2014, https://search.issuelab.org/resource/women-s-financial-inclusion-in-africa.html.

Karman (a journalist) for their efforts in championing women's rights and nonviolent activism in Liberia. Working through house arrest, imprisonment, and failure, President Sirleaf's achievements did not come easily.[24]

In the 1970s, when corporations would not promote Black women past middle management, some women started their own companies—and they took clients and talent with them. By the 1990s, these women-owned businesses were winning contracts from the same companies that had excluded them. Now, Black women are the fastest-growing business segment in the United States.[25] In Africa, Black women and Black men start businesses at roughly the same rate.[26]

In the Caribbean, from the time of enslavement, women's business trading helped create vibrant local economies. With their business activities in rural and urban areas, these women traveled to neighboring islands for commerce. Historians and anthropologists surmise that this practice must have been a legacy of their West African roots.[27] Jamaican market women, locked out of formal retail spaces, created cooperative buying and selling networks. These became the backbone of Caribbean commerce and influenced cooperative

---

24 "Ellen Johnson Sirleaf: Speed Read," The Nobel Prize, accessed January 12, 2026, https://www.nobelprize.org/prizes/peace/2011/johnson_sirleaf/speedread.

25 Morgan Smith, "Black Women Are the Fastest-Growing Group of Entrepreneurs in the US: Meet 3 Who Grew Their Side Hustles into Successful Businesses," *CNBC Make It*, February 18, 2024, https://www.cnbc.com/2024/02/18/black-women-are-the-fastest-growing-group-of-entrepreneurs-in-the-us.html.

26 Daniels, "Women's Financial Inclusion."

27 "Women Traders of the Caribbean," *Encyclopedia of African-American Culture and History*, accessed January 12, 2026, https://www.encyclopedia.com/history/encyclopedias-almanacs-transcripts-and-maps/women-traders-caribbean.

movements globally.[28] Today, Black women microbusiness owners are essential to their local and national economies and are an important success in international development.[29]

Black women have been forced to turn to microbusinesses, in part because banks won't lend them the money needed to start a business. When banks would not create inclusive banking policies to ease financial access to women in Kenya, Wangari Maathai and others created community savings groups that became the foundation for microfinance. These models spread across Africa and now serve millions of women worldwide who were previously excluded from formal banking.[30]

In the early twentieth century, when banks in the US refused loans to Black women, Maggie Lena Walker didn't just complain; she founded the first bank in the United States chartered by a Black woman. The St. Luke Penny Savings Bank became a model for other communities across the country.[31]

In 1995, Ursula Burns, a New York–born corporate executive, was stuck in a mid-level engineering role at Xerox. The traditional path to executive leadership wasn't working. So, she created her own. She started showing up to meetings she wasn't invited to. She volunteered for projects nobody wanted. She built relationships across departments instead of just climbing her own ladder. Everyone thought she

---

28 William Tantam, "Higgler Tactics: Techniques of Intermediary Market Traders in Jamaica," *Journal of Latin American and Caribbean Anthropology* 24, no. 1 (2019): 70–87, https://doi.org/10.1111/jlca.12360.

29 Winnifred Brown-Glaude, *Higglers in Kingston: Women's Informal Work in Jamaica* (Vanderbilt University Press, 2011).

30 "Wangari Maathai," Green Belt Movement, accessed January 12, 2026, https://www.greenbeltmovement.org/wangari-maathai.

31 Ahsan Washington, "Ten Black Women Who Broke Barriers in Business," *Black Enterprise*, March 12, 2025, https://www.blackenterprise.com/10-black-women-who-broke-barriers-in-business.

was doing it wrong. Twenty years later, Burns became the first Black woman CEO of a Fortune 500 company.

These women were all Revolutionary Pathmakers.

Revolutionary Systems' Navigation and Transformation

Your success depends on your strategy and implementation as you operate within a given system or context. Here are some of the strategies Black women have employed to overcome these barriers.

OUTSIDE-IN STRATEGY

As discussed, the outside-in strategy is about leveraging church networks, sorority connections, and community organizations for business relationships.

COALITION BUILDING

Traditional change efforts focus on convincing senior leadership. Revolutionary approaches build coalitions that include administrative staff, mid-level managers, and frontline workers. When change has support at every level, it becomes harder to resist and easier to implement.

DATA-DRIVEN DISRUPTION

Systems resist change when it feels like opinion. They can't resist facts. Revolutionary approaches gather evidence that makes problems impossible to ignore. Promotion rates by demographic. Pay gaps within similar roles. Retention data. Exit interview patterns. The numbers tell a story that is harder to dismiss than individual complaints.

Data also protects the messenger. When a Black woman presents evidence rather than grievances, the conversation shifts. She's not angry. She's the professional pointing out what the matrix reveals. The facts do the disrupting; she maintains credibility.

PARALLEL SYSTEMS CREATION

Rather than waiting for broken systems to be fixed, revolutionary leaders build alternative pathways that work alongside existing structures. These parallel systems often prove more effective and eventually replace the original systems.

STRATEGIC VISIBILITY CAMPAIGNS

Revolutionary transformation requires making invisible barriers visible. This means documenting microaggressions, showcasing talent that's been overlooked, and creating platforms that highlight the gap between stated values and actual practices.

RESOURCE REALLOCATION

Revolutionary leaders identify where power actually flows in organizations and redirect resources toward more inclusive approaches. This might mean shifting the budget from ineffective diversity training to mentorship programs that produce measurable results.

CULTURAL PROOF POINTS

Instead of arguing for change in theory, revolutionary leaders create small-scale demonstrations that prove new approaches work better. These become proof points that make larger transformations inevitable.

KEY TAKEAWAYS

- Having family responsibilities positively impacts your achievements in the workplace.
- Success at both home and work is possible and statistically attainable.
- Though exclusionary systems exist, you can find a solution around them.
- Exclusionary systems are designed to impede your advancement, but they are your secret weapon for massive advancement.
- Don't be afraid to come up with innovative solutions.

ACTION STEPS

- Write down a list of systems you feel exclude you in the workplace. Identify the top two or three and consider what you can do to thrive in this system regardless.
- Draft a list of your active social circles, and choose one or two to consistently contribute more to.

CHAPTER 3

Revolutionary from the Outside In

We teach girls to shrink themselves, to make themselves smaller.
CHIMAMANDA NGOZI ADICHIE

In the previous chapter, we discussed the systemic barriers or exclusionary systems that negatively impact Black women and their success. In this chapter, we broaden the perspective to the societal contexts shaping Black women's leadership.

POWER ACTIVATION PROMPT

Think about a leadership approach you have used that others once questioned but now everyone seems to be adopting. What circumstances or experiences allowed you to be ahead of the curve?

Historical Context and Evolution

Black women's leadership has been shaped by multifaceted and interconnected political, economic, and cultural factors. Exclusion from education and from civic and workforce participation meant that Black women were forced to develop alternative power structures and innovative leadership approaches.

Let us take a brief look at how, historically, Black women have managed to creatively problem solve during difficult situations.

PRE–TWENTIETH CENTURY

During enslavement, Black women such as Harriet Tubman created the Underground Railroad network. This network was an ingenious device that allowed Black people to find their way to freedom utilizing covert communication systems, trust-building methodologies, and high-stakes decision-making under extreme pressure.

After emancipation, Black people needed to build institutions that catered to our express needs. Pioneers realized that fundraising was necessary, and to maximize finances, it had to be done across racial and political barriers. This fundraising had to be done without formal power or authority for what was considered forbidden: educating the uneducated—Black people.

Mary McLeod Bethune is one such Revolutionary Pathmaker in the space of civil and women's rights and education for Black people. Her revolutionary leadership helped shape the standards of Black college education that are maintained to this day. She proved Black colleges could maintain academic rigor while addressing students' economic hardships. She established that Black colleges should be led by Black educators who understood their students' experiences, not by white administrators who imposed assumptions. Among her many ground-breaking achievements, Bethune also founded the National Council of Negro Women (NCNW)[32] and served as an advisor to President Franklin Roosevelt, advocating for African American matters.

In Nigeria in 1932, Funmilayo Ransome-Kuti helped set up a ladies' club that, over time, evolved into a national organization called the Federation of Nigerian Women's Societies. Through this organization, Ransome-Kuti and her fellow Nigerian women campaigned around a variety of issues impacting their lives and businesses, such as price controls and special taxes that impoverished market women, and advocated for more educational opportunities, sanitary policies, healthcare, and social services.[33]

TWENTIETH CENTURY

In the Jim Crow era, Black women's parallel institution-building activities developed efficient organizational management, creative resource allocation, and sustainable community development approaches. Black women also created mutual aid networks and professional development systems outside white-only or mainstream structures.

During the civil rights era, the integration of legal strategy with grassroots organization created comprehensive change methodologies. These approaches balanced both immediate action and long-term infrastructure building. Revolutionary Pathmaker Dorothy Height is worth highlighting here for her many efforts in activism and the empowerment of Black people. Through her work with the NCNW, she helped end lynching across the USA and fought for change in the criminal justice system. During her four decades of leadership of the

32 Debra Michals (ed.), "Mary McLeod Bethune," National Women's History Museum, 2015, https://www.womenshistory.org/education-resources/biographies/mary-mcleod-bethune.

33 "Funmilayo Ransome-Kuti," in *Encyclopaedia Britannica*, last modified October 21, 2025, https://www.britannica.com/biography/Funmilayo-Ransome-Kuti.

NCNW, she also supported voter registration for Black citizens and funded several civil rights activists.[34]

In Kenya, Revolutionary Pathmaker Wangari Maathai was the first East African woman to attain a PhD from the University of Kenya, where she also championed equal work benefits for her fellow women employed at the university. She also established a tree-planting initiative called the Green Belt Movement, which involved a hundred thousand women.[35] Between 1977 and 2005, her initiative planted over thirty million trees.[36]

TWENTY-FIRST CENTURY

Despite the rampant gendered racism in online spaces, when it comes to digital access, Black women have leveraged traditional community-building skills to foster social media organizations that have created global movements using grassroots principles.[37]

Black Lives Matter, which was started in 2013 by three Revolutionary Pathmakers—Alicia Garza, Patrisse Cullors, and Opal Tometi—is grounded in the digital. From July 2020 to June 2021, blacklivesmatter.com received nearly forty million visitors from around the world, allowing the movement to leverage community

34 Arlisha Norwood, "Dorothy Height," National Women's History Museum, 2017, https://www.womenshistory.org/education-resources/biographies/dorothy-height.

35 Cora Ann Presley, "Women's Empowerment: The Insights of Wangari Maathai," *Forum Philosophicum* 18, no. 2 (2013): 243–53, https://doi.org/10.1080/17449626.2013.856640.

36 Mia MacDonald, "The Green Belt Movement, and the Story of Wangari Maathai," *YES! Magazine*, March 26, 2005, https://www.yesmagazine.org/issue/media/2005/03/26/the-green-belt-movement-the-story-of-wangari-maathai.

37 Tykeia Robinson and Brittany Williams, "Still Retaining Each Other: Black Women Building Community Through Social Media and Other Digital Platforms," in *Investing in the Educational Success of Black Women and Girls*, ed. Lori D. Patton et al. (Routledge, 2022), 258–75.

power in several ways, including raising financial support and petitioning leaders in power.[38]

The Me Too movement, often credited to Revolutionary Pathmaker Tarana Burke,[39] came into prominence in 2017, drawing the world's attention to widespread allegations of sexual misconduct in the workplace. It was a trend. One monumental development from this powerful social justice movement was the abolishment of the statute of limitations for sexual criminal acts and the banning of nondisclosure agreements intended to silence survivors.[40]

To address health disparities, Revolutionary Pathmakers such as Professor Camara Phyllis Jones engage in community-based health advocacy that uses medical knowledge and cultural competence to create approaches that address systemic health barriers. Her organization also provides immediate community support.[41] Another Revolutionary Pathmaker in the healthcare field is Kizzmekia S. Corbett-Helaire. Corbett-Helaire was one of the scientists who contributed significantly to the development of the Moderna COVID-19 vaccine. She led a team at the National Institutes of Health that was responsible for vaccine research, designing a vaccine with a 94 percent success rate.[42]

---

38 *2020–2021 Impact Report* (Black Lives Matter Global Network Foundation, 2023), https://impact.blacklivesmatter.com/wp-content/uploads/2023/03/BLMGNF-Impact-Report-2020-2021.pdf.

39 "Tarana Burke," in *Encyclopedia Britannica*, last modified September 8, 2025, https://www.britannica.com/biography/Tarana-Burke.

40 Amy Brittain, "Me Too Movement," in *Encyclopedia Britannica*, last modified January 8, 2026, https://www.britannica.com/topic/Me-Too-movement.

41 "Camara Jones," Emory University, Rollins School of Public Health, accessed January 13, 2026, https://sph.emory.edu/profile/faculty/camara-jones.

42 "Honoring Dr. Kizzmekia Corbett," The Oregon Clinic, February 10, 2025, https://www.oregonclinic.com/newsroom/honoring-dr-kizzmekia-corbett.

Black women have spearheaded economic innovation through entrepreneurship and alternative career paths, using community networks and creative financing to build businesses that serve overlooked markets while creating community wealth. They have also used creative financing, such as early forms of crowdsourcing, bootstrapping and personal investments, and minority-owned banks to achieve their ends.

South Africa's Phumzile Mlambo-Ngcuka, a former executive director of United Nations Women, helped champion women's economic empowerment by advocating for the elimination of financial access limitations and encouraging entrepreneurship.[43] As the deputy president of South Africa,[44] Mlambo-Ngcuka backed policies designed to help usher South Africa into a more economically inclusive society. Bethlehem Tilahun Alemu, from Ethiopia, is the founder of soleRebels, a fast-growing footwear company that has created over a hundred thousand jobs and USD 1 billion in revenue.[45]

These contributions made by Revolutionary Pathmakers have provided job creation opportunities, financial literacy, advocacy and representation, and inspiration for future generations.

Transition from Radical to Mainstream

Black women exercise distinctive leadership styles, typically characterized as collaborative, community-centered, and resilient. This leader-

43 "Ms. Mlambo-Ngcuka, Phumzile," United Nations Department of Economic and Social Affairs, accessed January 13, 2026, https://sdgs.un.org/panelists/ms-mlambo-ngcuka-phumzile-29103.

44 "Former Deputy President Phumzile Mlambo-Ngcuka," The Presidency, Republic of South Africa, accessed January 13, 2026, https://www.gov.za/about-government/contact-directory/phumzile-mlambo-ngcuka-ms.

45 "2022 Laureate: Bethlehem Tilahun Alemu," Global Business Hall of Fame, accessed January 13, 2026, https://www.businesshalloffame.org/bethlehem-tilahun-alemu.

ship style prioritizes decision-making through consensus building and inclusive participation rather than top-down authority.

Successful collaborative efforts require authentic communication, which involves the integration of personal values with professional responsibilities. It requires vulnerable leadership that acknowledges uncertainty and admits to not having all the answers while still maintaining direction.

Being community-centered means prioritizing collective advancement alongside individual success, not over it or in competition with it. Sustainable progress requires lifting others and bringing them along, not being a lone warrior.

To engage adaptive resilience, another facet of revolutionary leadership, Black women allow their methods to be flexible while they maintain consistent core values that are grounded in meaningful prioritization. A resilient leader can pivot strategies based on changing circumstances without undermining their larger goals.

Black Women's Leadership Today

Through seminal works by brain and behavior experts such as Daniel Goleman, significant attention has been paid to the notions of emotional intelligence[46] and social intelligence.[47]

Emotional intelligence is the ability to both recognize and manage your own emotions and to understand and influence the emotions of others. Social intelligence is the ability to navigate complex social situations and build effective relationships. In recent decades, these have both become recognized as core leadership competencies.

---

46 Daniel Goleman, *Emotional Intelligence* (Bantam Books, 1997).

47 Daniel Goleman, *Social Intelligence: The New Science of Human Relationships* (Bantam Books, 2007).

But Black women have practiced these skills for generations, out of necessity. Reading a room to assess safety. Managing emotions to avoid being labeled "angry." Building trust across differences to create coalitions. Navigating power dynamics while maintaining authenticity. These weren't optional leadership development courses. They were survival requirements that became sophisticated leadership approaches long before corporate America gave them official names and frameworks.

Stakeholder capitalism, which prioritizes community impact alongside profit, is another trend that aligns with Black women's leadership because it reflects the community-centered values Black women have always practiced. This approach is typified by solving challenges for the most impacted.

Another hallmark of Black women's leadership style is being purpose driven. This means integrating personal missions with professional work. Black women often refuse to separate who they are from what they do, even when that refusal costs them advancement opportunities.

This approach validates itself when organizations demand value compromises for career growth. A Black woman who leads with purpose won't abandon her community connections to fit corporate culture. She won't pretend systemic problems don't exist to make leadership comfortable. She won't perform a version of herself that denies her lived experience. Her authentic leadership becomes the standard, not the compromise.

Lastly, crisis leadership, which came into great and global significance during the COVID-19 pandemic, is emblematic of approaches that Black women have used throughout the ages. Successful crisis leadership requires empathy, a tolerance for uncertainty, and team connection. This style of leadership borrows from and validates approaches Black women have used in resource-constrained environments, often to beat incredible odds.

RECOGNITION

Through academic integration, corporate implementation, and the consulting industry, Black women's leadership strategies are being adopted and recognized. Business schools are now teaching inclusive leadership, cultural competence, and emotional intelligence as core business and MBA competencies.

In the corporate world, including in Fortune 500 companies, collaborative decision-making, values-based leadership, and community engagement strategies have been widely adopted—and not just for "specialty" or "innovative" business groups, but as standard practices.

In the consulting industry, the leadership development market increasingly packages approaches that Black women developed through lived experience, driving the commercial demand for these methodologies.

Connecting Individual Experience to Collective Patterns

When we consider the individual Black woman's experience and how this reflects collective leadership patterns, we come to realize how personal innovation, when systematized, can transform entire leadership paradigms. Black women's individual responses to exclusion and constraint created and continue to create the collective wisdom that is now recognized as essential for organizational success in complex, rapidly changing environments. *However, it is also important for Black women to lead these transformations and not be used as models and then* negotiated *out when others can* emulate *what we've perfected.* To connect individual experiences to collective patterns, devices such as personal stories, shared patterns, and other mechanisms provide insights and invaluable knowledge.

PERSONAL STORIES

The personal stories of Black women hold the common themes of early responsibility, cultural navigation, and value integration. From childhood, Black women must often support or manage family and community dynamics. Through these efforts, we have developed crisis management, multitasking, and protective leadership qualities.

Black women exercise nimble cultural navigation across multiple contexts. This includes code-switching, the act of adjusting language, behavior, or appearance to fit a different social setting while maintaining authenticity. This means adopting white professional norms at work and reverting to authentic communication in other spaces. This constant adjustment allows Black women to develop sophisticated social intelligence: reading environments, understanding unspoken rules, and adapting without losing their core identity. While this fluidity allows Black women to advance in educational and professional pursuits, the mental cost goes unacknowledged.

Value integration is another theme that runs through Black women's personal experiences. Achieving long-term effectiveness requires finding ways to align personal values, lifestyles, and familial and caregiving responsibilities with professional responsibilities, rather than compartmentalizing these aspects.

SHARED PATTERNS

Individual experiences contribute to broader leadership trends through strategic relationship building, institutional influence, and cultural transformation. Strategic relationship building or network effects occur when individual success creates opportunities for others through mentorship, sponsorship, and cultural bridge building. This gradually normalizes different leadership approaches.

Institutional influence occurs when well-executed personal leadership styles effectively demonstrate more effective ways of operating, allowing for the transformation of organizational cultures.

Successful leaders have brought community-developed approaches into different types of organizational environments, whether corporate, nonprofit, government, or otherwise, gradually encouraging the acceptance of alternative leadership styles and methods and culminating in cultural transformation.

MECHANISMS

Mechanisms already in place in organizations, such as mentorship, connect stories to collective impact. Mentorship networks provide both formal and informal navigation and guidance that allow for the transmission of new leadership methods.

Individual leaders in influential positions implemented policies and practices that embedded community-developed approaches into organizational structures, and professional organizations and affinity groups created platforms for these sharing strategies, building collective influence. Cultural documentation, such as personal narratives, academic research, and media representation, have helped to systematize and legitimize these approaches, creating lasting systemic and institutional change.

KEY TAKEAWAYS

- Document all the new and radical approaches you take. One of these could be the next leadership strategy that will help you lead your team through uncertain times.
- Constraint-driven approaches often can and will rise to the top.
- The wisdom you develop because of your experiences translates into the workplace. Your family and friend networks are not separate from your professional competencies.
- Validation doesn't require permission; you don't need corporate endorsement to implement your approaches. Timing is everything in terms of making the approach an essential rather than an alternative one.

ACTION STEPS

- Audit your revolutionary approaches: Identify what others have dismissed or questioned. Consider where you've learned these approaches. Was it from your community, your family, or necessity? Note situations where these have proven to be more successful than traditional approaches.
- Research: Do a simple online search on leadership trends that align with your approaches. Note if and where your approaches have created different outcomes.

CHAPTER 4
The Revolutionary Power of Care

Strong people don't need strong leaders.
ELLA BAKER

What is meant by the concept of care? People often imagine care to be "women's work," but the truth is, it isn't—everyone can act with care. Care can simply be described as actions characterized by kindness. And while we often think of leadership as command and control, in-your-face, and aggressive, it can—and should—be kind. Care, in its full complexity, is an aspect of strategic leadership. It encapsulates community, protection, and transformation. It's an approach that prioritizes humanity and human kindness.

A GALLON OF MILK A DAY

Mothering is a practice of transformation. We are transformed as we transform the world through the work of caring.
ALEXIS PAULINE GUMBS

An email arrived at ten minutes to midnight in the middle of the week. It was another "urgent" analysis needing my immediate attention, despite having no real deadline. I stared at my phone while pumping breast milk for my infant twins, my mind half on alert in case my babies started crying over the baby monitor.

My colleague's message was matter-of-fact: "Can you jump on this ASAP? I know you are just easing in from maternity leave, so not back to full speed yet." Easing in? I'd been "eased in" well before I'd planned to be and should have been.

I had spent the last month managing a team in crisis, facilitating a difficult strategic partnership, and developing an implementation strategy for an upcoming initiative that required a lot of buy-in. On top of that, I had to produce over a gallon of milk a day while also nursing infants on demand, coordinating childcare, preparing to return to a demanding job, managing medical appointments, supporting two adult kids, and somehow keeping a household running. But according to workplace thinking, only one of these categories counted as "real work."

This moment crystallized something I'd experienced twenty years earlier and observed through my career. The same caring responsibility that others viewed as a distraction or limitation had actually developed some of my most powerful leadership capa-

bilities. Capabilities such as emotional intelligence, resource management, and protective instinct.

Emotional intelligence was required to grow, feed, and care for two infants simultaneously while leading a large-scale organizational transformation. Resource management skills were needed to coordinate multiple caregivers across different schedules, in different cities and time zones, while managing project timelines and supporting the launch of my two adult children. Protective instincts drove me to advocate fiercely for my children, which translated directly to advocating for my team members.

POWER ACTIVATION PROMPT

Consider how your care responsibilities have led to you developing leadership skills that others might not recognize as professional assets.

Research Validation

The research offers deeper insights into the revolutionary power of care—not as sentiment or softness, but as a form of strategic leadership labor. Across both my 2010[48] and 2025[49] studies, care consistently emerged as a meaningful and identity-shaping dimension of Black women's purpose-driven leadership and responsibilities and their experience of success.

But the newer analysis also reveals a harder truth: While care strengthens connection, resilience, and stability within organizations

48 Jones, "Quantitative Study."

49 Brown, "Revolutionary Evidence."

and communities, the systems surrounding Black women rarely share the cost of that labor.

In organizational settings, women with heavier caregiving responsibilities were less likely to experience upward mobility over time—even when they were already in leadership roles. Among entrepreneurs, caregiving was associated with slower business growth and lower satisfaction, particularly in the years following COVID-19, as women carried both economic risk and relational responsibility. These findings do not suggest that caregiving weakens leadership. Instead, they show that care is often performed inside environments that are not structurally designed to support it.

Care-centered leaders hold teams together, absorb emotional strain, mentor across generations, and stabilize institutions during disruption—and yet the reward system around them rarely accounts for that burden. The question, then, is not whether Black women lead powerfully through care but why the systems that benefit from that care so rarely invest in its sustainability.

Organizational Benefits

Care-driven leaders bring undeniable value to organizations. Leaders grounded in care foster trust, protect team morale during change, and create spaces where people feel seen, supported, and accountable to one another. These are the conditions under which innovation, belonging, and ethical decision-making become possible.

But the research makes it clear that these strengths do not absolve systems of responsibility.[50]

Too often, Black women network less, but not because they are disengaged; rather, they are networking strategically because time,

50 Jones, "Quantitative Study."

caregiving, and emotional labor require precision rather than excess. What appears from the outside as efficiency is, in many cases, survival-based discernment. Care-centered leaders are not performing less—they are carrying more, and they are doing so in ways that must be both acknowledged and supported.

Leadership does not pause when Black women leave the office or close a laptop. Care extends across family, community, faith, entrepreneurship, and organizational life. It is not a private obligation—it is a form of labor that sustains institutions even when institutions do not fully sustain the people who perform it.

This is what makes care revolutionary. Not because it transforms how we lead—but because it exposes what must change in the systems we lead within.

Historical Context

Black women have cared for others throughout the ages, within family and gender roles. These responsibilities span child-rearing, care for the elderly, and spousal or extended family support, but they also include managing resources, allocating budgets across competing household needs, and planning strategically for family goals. Revolutionary Pathmakers grasp the importance of empathy and understanding as well as strategy in care management. These women know that life is not just about their work but about balancing work with family care management and household leadership.

Black women's approach to care does not emanate from any leadership theory. Rather, it has been developed through centuries of protecting and developing Black communities under extreme constraints.

Because they were often excluded from mainstream solutions, in the United States, Black communities created systems, and organizations and groups such as the Free African Society and the Independent Order of St. Luke emerged. The Free African Society gave aid to former enslaved persons who needed support to get on their feet.[51] The Independent Order of St. Luke, founded by former enslaved woman Mary Prout, offered a level of social security, including mutual aid and even burial benefits for its members.[52] Black churches, often under the guidance of Black women congregants, offered not only a spiritual, emotional, and religious support system but also invaluable services to their communities, such as venues for education, political mobilization, and community activism.[53]

During the Jim Crow era, Black neighborhoods such as the one found in Tulsa, Oklahoma, thrived through their own Black businesses and insulated economies. Tulsa flourished even during the Great Depression, with one area, Greenwood, coming to be known as Black Wall Street. Tragically, the area was destroyed during the Tulsa race massacre.[54] This era also marked a turning point in Black cultural development, establishing foundations that continue to shape Black culture today.

There were also Black-owned schools, universities and colleges, and networking groups that existed to serve and support Black people. The Rosenwald schools in the rural South helped educate young

---

51 "The Free African Society," Richard Allen, Apostle of Freedom [exhibition], Historical Society of Pennsylvania, accessed January 13, 2026, https://hsp.org/history-online/exhibits/richard-allen-apostle-of-freedom/the-free-african-society.

52 "Independent Order of St. Luke," National Museum of African American History and Culture, accessed January 13, 2026, https://www.searchablemuseum.com/independent-order-of-st-luke.

53 Nicole Myers Turner, "Beyond Speeches and Leaders: The Role of Black Churches in the Reconstruction of the United States," *Journal of the Civil War Era*, August 14, 2020, https://www.journalofthecivilwarera.org/2020/08/beyond-speeches-and-leaders-the-role-of-black-churches-in-the-reconstruction-of-the-united-states.

54 "Black Wall Street," in *Encyclopedia Britannica*, last modified December 6, 2025, https://www.britannica.com/place/Black-Wall-Street.

Black people, some of whom went on to become powerful civil rights leaders. With approximately five thousand Rosenwald schools, many young people were educated and became literate.[55] Universities and colleges, such as Historically Black Colleges and Universities, which initially offered training to people to become teachers or traders, have become far more sophisticated and expansive over time.[56]

Similarly, across the world, Black communities have historically found ways to support and care for one another under extraordinary circumstances, through the colonial era and continued imperialist oppression. Countries such as Jamaica[57] and Bermuda provided aid to those in need through friendly societies, voluntary organizations that supported members financially and socially.[58]

Ethiopia's resistance against Italian colonial oppression made such a profound impression on Africans across the continent that it successfully challenged the false stereotype that Africans are inferior to their former colonizers. Churches such as the Ethiopian Church were impactful both religiously and politically, with some churches even facilitating the resistance against colonial rule and the formation of indigenous leadership structures to overcome the country's imperialist overlords.[59]

---

55 "Rosenwald Schools," in *Encyclopedia Britannica,* last modified September 2, 2025, https://www.britannica.com/topic/Rosenwald-schools.

56 "Historically Black Colleges and Universities," in *Encyclopedia Britannica,* last modified January 7, 2026, https://www.britannica.com/topic/historically-black-colleges-and-universities.

57 "About Us," The Department of Co-operatives and Friendly Societies, accessed January 13, 2026, https://www.dcfs.gov.jm/aboutUs.html.

58 Heather Campbell, "Friendly Society," in *Britannica Money,* accessed January 13, 2026, https://www.britannica.com/money/friendly-society.

59 Mammo Muchie, "The Relevance of Ethiopianism to Africa Today," presentation, Human Sciences Research Council Seminar, Pretoria, Durban, and Cape Town, May 17, 2013, https://hsrc.ac.za/uploads/pageContent/3371/EthiopianismHSRCf.pdf.

In some ways, Freetown in Sierra Leone stands out as an interesting parallel to Tulsa's Black Wall Street. Freetown was established in 1787 as a home for freed enslaved people who had been left completely destitute after attaining their freedom. Former enslaved persons from England were among the first to make their new home in Freetown. They were followed by others from Nova Scotia, who gained their freedom after fighting on the side of the British; former enslaved men, women, and children from Jamaica fleeing oppression; and those rescued from captured enslavement ships.[60] Though Freetown was an imperfect destination, it was a haven in a world where Black people's freedoms and very existence were precarious.

Care as a Leadership Development Laboratory

In current times, our responsibilities and access to one another are different from previous eras. With this understanding, and the support of modern research, organizations are beginning to catch on too. This has been an exceptional development, since qualified women of childbearing age were often sidelined (and, too often, still are) from opportunities they were qualified for because of the anticipated disruption or adjustments associated with child-rearing. With over 80 percent of women in the USA ultimately becoming mothers,[61] this sidelining has serious consequences for the workforce. The research is clear: There is significant leadership potential among the transferable

60 "Freetown," in *Encyclopedia Britannica*, last modified August 14, 2023, https://www.britannica.com/place/Freetown.

61 Sarah Pruitt, "How U.S. Employers Have Handled Pregnancy in the Workplace," *History*, October 17, 2019, https://www.history.com/articles/pregnancy-workplace-employers-federal-government.

skills women possess, honed from their motherhood experiences.[62] One study shows that some of the transferable skills from their care roles (such as parenting) to their careers include "more interpersonal, time management, and problem-solving skills."[63] Another study found multitasking, time management, emotional intelligence, enhanced cognitive ability, and increased willpower to be those transferable skills. I have also noticed that community-centered leadership is an invaluable skill that these women develop through the complexities of motherhood and other care roles they fill.

WE'RE IN THE LAB

Don't wait around for other people to be happy for you.
Any happiness you get, you've got to make yourself.
ALICE WALKER

As a mother of four and a wife, I engage in a variety of daily leadership tasks, such as strategically planning for my family at the beginning of every week. At some point, I realized these relate or are identical to the leadership tasks I undertake for work.

I also realized that each broader context was much like a laboratory—a care laboratory. It became clear to me that this was not just family management; it was training—training in how

62 Emily Ma et al., "On the Bright Side of Motherhood—A Mixed Method Enquiry," *Annals of Tourism Research* 92 (2022): 103350, https://doi.org/10.1016/j.annals.2022.103350.

63 Ana Júlia Calegari Torres et al., "The Impact of Motherhood on Women's Career Progression: A Scoping Review of Evidence-Based Interventions," *Behavioral Sciences* 14, no. 4 (2024): 275, https://doi.org/10.3390/bs14040275.

> *to get those tasks done while simultaneously advancing in my career. Juggling the competing yet important responsibilities of managing a household while advancing in my career, completing a degree program, and working full-time required the same types of competencies that MBA programs are trying to develop in students. These competencies included strategic thinking, business management, resource optimization, and managing stakeholders.*

The research consistently reveals a pattern: Black women who maintained strong family and community care responsibilities often demonstrated superior leadership capabilities compared with those who didn't have this experience.[64]

Community Care as an Organizational Model

The core of community care as an organizational model is the emphasis on collective over individual responsibility and achievement. In this model, we care about group success more than individual acclaim. From traditional wisdom, we are taught that genuine success requires that we lift everyone up. This stands in opposition to systems that seek individual advancement at the expense of others. Community care sees the value of group input and is against the idea of negotiating others out of the acknowledgment they have earned. The organic collective approach outperforms the alternative because it makes for sustainable success, building stronger, more resilient organizations.

The beauty of community care as an organizational model is its focus on collective growth and team building. A manager employing this organizational model is likely to lead through a mentorship and

---

64 Jones, "Quantitative Study."

personnel development stance when it comes to engaging with team members. These managers do not just want others to listen and do as they're told; they want the team to build their capacity over time and further their impact and success. Such managers also reflect on their interactions with their team, and they use those experiences—both positive and negative—as data points for the continued growth and honing of their managerial skills. Revolutionary Pathmakers do not hoard knowledge; rather, they prioritize knowledge transfer.

KEY TAKEAWAYS

- Care responsibilities are foundational and create highly sophisticated leadership competencies, such as emotional intelligence, crisis management, and resource optimization.
- This has been demonstrated through historical patterns throughout enslavement; post emancipation, Jim Crow, civil rights, and affirmative action; and even still today.
- These historical patterns show that these care approaches were developed through necessity.
- Community care principles create better organizational outcomes than individual or traditional ones.
- Engaging in care work enhances, rather than diminishes, Black women's leadership.

ACTION STEPS

- Identify specific leadership competencies you have developed or gained through care responsibilities.

- Practice describing your care experience as executive development rather than as a professional challenge.
- Pick a community care approach and apply its practices or principles to a current professional challenge.

CHAPTER 5

Community as Leadership Incubator

I believe unconditionally in the ability of people to respond when they are told the truth. We need to be taught to study rather than believe, to inquire rather than to affirm.

SEPTIMA CLARK

In this chapter, we shift our focus to the community as a *leadership incubator*: that is, to how the community provides the ideal conditions for leadership skills to naturally develop, offering real responsibilities and meaningful stakes that have real impact on diverse stakeholders. The community offers immediate feedback, with community support and cultural alignment enabling experimentation and growth. This type of leadership incubator is typically not designed for your failure. This perspective is crucial, primarily because there are few leadership or experimentation opportunities for Black women. As such, leadership competencies must be developed before you get the opportunity to practice them in crucial career roles. Since Black women don't typically get tapped for potential, the role that the community offers is vital.

CASE STUDY: MAMA AFRICA

When Miriam [Makeba] recorded the hit version [of the song "Pata Pata"], she was pretty much a lone voice speaking out against apartheid and crucially making the world aware of the inhumanity of it … I think she understood the power of music, and used that power.

RITA RAY

Miriam Makeba was a Revolutionary Pathmaker who chose music as her vehicle of excellence. Born in South Africa in 1932, during the apartheid era, her illustrious career spanning five decades had her traveling the globe to spread her musical talent in traditional African song, earning her the nickname "Mama Africa." As a South African with Xhosa and Swazi roots, she developed a musical repertoire that showcased the richness and rhythm of South African culture.[65]

In 1963, when she was in her early thirties, she was invited to speak at the United Nations General Assembly. There, Makeba advocated for her fellow non-white South Africans and pleaded with the international community to compel the South African government to abolish apartheid.[66]

Makeba said at the General Assembly:

"I ask you and all the leaders of the world, would you act differently, would you keep silent and do nothing if you were in our place? Would you not resist if you were allowed no rights in

65 Ibid.

66 "Miriam Makeba's Historic Speech Remembered," *The World*, August 15, 2013, https://theworld.org/stories/2013/08/15/miriam-makebas-historic-speech-remembered.

your own country because the color of your skin is different from that of the rulers, and if you were punished for even asking for equality. I appeal to you, and to all the countries of the world to do everything you can to stop the coming tragedy. I appeal to you to save the lives of our leaders, to empty the prisons of all those who should never have been there."[67]

POWER ACTIVATION PROMPT

What leadership skills have you developed through church, community, or cultural organizations that you've never thought to put on your resume?

Historical Validation

There are a host of examples that validate the efficacy of communities as leadership incubators. Barbara Jordan,[68] Ursula Burns,[69] Mellody Hobson,[70]

67 Ibid.

68 "Jordan, Barbara Charline," in *Biographical Directory of the United States Congress*, accessed January 13, 2026, https://history.house.gov/People/Detail/16031.

69 Jeannette L. Nolen, "Ursula Burns," in *Britannica Money*, accessed January 13, 2026, https://www.britannica.com/money/Ursula-Burns.

70 "Mellody Hobson," The Rockefeller Foundation, accessed January 13, 2026, https://www.rockefellerfoundation.org/profiles/mellody-hobson.

Stacey Abrams,[71] Adese Okojie,[72] Glanis Changachirere,[73] Farida Charity,[74] Alice Banze,[75] and Dr. Joanna Abeyie[76] are a few examples of community leaders who translated to organizational leaders.

A Zimbabwean activist and founding coordinator of the African Women Leaders Forum, Glanis Changachirere was moved to start her organization, the Institute for Young Women Development, at only twenty-six years old. She wanted to help young women rise above the limitations in her country of Zimbabwe. She rebelled against the societal expectation that girls do not advance in the same way boys do and therefore do not deserve the same rights and opportunities. At present, her organization has over seven thousand members, and it works with other national bodies to impact Zimbabwean policy, such as the Gender Equality Bill.[77]

Born in 1936 in Texas, Barbara Jordan became a practicing lawyer in 1960.[78] In 1967, she became the first Black woman state senator in Texas.[79]

Ursula Burns was the second-born child of a single mother who ran a home-based day care service as her main source of income.

---

71 "Stacey Abrams," in *Encyclopedia Britannica*, last modified December 5, 2025, https://www.britannica.com/biography/Stacey-Abrams.

72 "#STRETCH25: Top 25 Black and Ethnically Diverse Women Advancing Equity, Diversity and Inclusion in Corporate UK 2023," *Career Masterclass*, accessed September 15, 2025, https://careermasterclass.com/stretch25-ethnically-diverse-women.

73 "Ten African Women Leaders We Admire," *Africa UN Women*, March 10, 2021, https://africa.unwomen.org/en/news-and-events/stories/2021/03/ten-african-women-leaders-we-admire.

74 Ibid.

75 Ibid.

76 *Career Masterclass*, "#STRETCH25."

77 Ibid.

78 Ibid.

79 Ibid.

Wanting her daughter to attain the very best education she could, Burns's mother also took on cleaning and ironing chores so she could afford to send her daughter to a preparatory school, where she excelled, particularly in mathematics. She went on to attain a master's degree in engineering and then began her career at Xerox as an intern. Through her hard work, Burns rose through the ranks, eventually becoming the company's first Black female CEO—and, in fact, the first Black CEO of a Fortune 500 company.[80]

Mellody Hobson, another leader who emerged from a single-parent home, was one of six siblings. Seeing her mother's financial struggles instilled in her a resolve to rise from poverty, master financial management, and take others with her by helping them gain financial literacy. Her desire for a career in finance led her to excel academically and earn an Ivy League education at Princeton, after which she began working at Ariel Investments. In 2019, she was appointed CEO; she became president of Ariel Investments in 2020. Hobson has credited her family's financial hardship for her success in life.[81]

Skill Translation Framework

How do we translate the skills we develop in our communities into skills we can confidently and effectively use throughout our working careers? This is where my three-part *Skills Translation Framework* (or *Processes*) comes in.

80 Nolen, "Ursula Burns."

81 Daniel Liberto, "Who Is Mellody Hobson?," *Investopedia*, last modified February 15, 2024, https://www.investopedia.com/who-is-mellody-hobson-5217368.

1. MAPPING COMMUNITY ROLES TO LEADERSHIP COMPETENCIES

Take out a piece of paper, and draw two columns. On the left, list your community roles and activities. On the right, identify the leadership competency each one develops.

REAL EXAMPLES:

COMMUNITY ROLE	LEADERSHIP COMPETENCY
Church finance community member	Budget management and fiscal oversight
Youth basketball coach	Team development and performance management
Neighborhood association organizer	Stakeholder engagement and project management
Family reunion planning committee	Event coordination and multigenerational communication
Sorority chapter president	Strategic planning and volunteer leadership
Sunday school teacher	Curriculum development and adult education facilitation

YOUR TURN

List three to five significant community roles you've held. For each one, ask, "What skills did this require?" Then translate those skills into leadership language.

2. HOW TO SPEAK OF COMMUNITY EXPERIENCE IN PROFESSIONAL TERMS

This isn't about changing what you did—it's about making the value crystal clear. Here's the formula:

[Action Verb] + [Specific Task]
+ [Measurable Result] + [Leadership Context]

Before (underselling): "I help out with my church's finances."

After (leadership translation): "Managed a $250,000 annual budget for a five-hundred-member organization, implementing financial controls that reduced discrepancies by 40 percent and improved quarterly reporting accuracy."

Before: "I organized our family reunion."

After: "Coordinated a multistate event for 150 participants, managing vendor relationships, budget allocation, and intergenerational communication across four time zones."

Before: "I mentor young people in my neighborhood."

After: "Provided strategic guidance and skill development to twelve emerging professionals, resulting in eight college acceptances and three promotions within eight months."

The confidence component: Notice how the "after" versions don't apologize, minimize, or use qualifiers such as "just" or "volunteered." Your community work *is* leadership experience. Own it completely.

3. HOW TO LAY OUT THE EVIDENCE

Create your evidence portfolio:

For each translated skill, gather concrete proof.

Quantitative evidence:

- Budget sizes you've managed
- Number of people you've led or served
- Measurable outcomes (percentage increase, number of participants, funds raised)
- Timing of consistent engagement

Qualitative evidence:

- Testimonials from community members
- Documentation of programs you've created
- Photos/materials for events you've organized
- Awards or recognition received

Example evidence package:

Skill claim: "Experienced in change management and stakeholder engagement."

Supporting evidence:

- Led a neighborhood improvement initiative that increased resident participation from 12 percent to 67 percent over two years.
- Managed resistance to new policies by conducting fifteen listening sessions with over two hundred community members.
- Secured buy-in from eight different community groups with competing priorities.
- Provided a testimony from a city council member citing your collaborative approach.
- Provided before-and-after photos showing tangible neighborhood improvements.

Cultural Capital Recognition

It's worth taking a moment here to make a professional assessment of community networks because as much as the individual offers human capital, which is their individual competency, so too does the community. The community and its members have a symbiotic relationship. At the same time, we also need to explore cultural competence as a competitive advantage to the global workforce and our businesses. Naturally, the competencies of the community vary because we are all part of different communities, each of which comes with its own culture.

PROFESSIONAL ASSESSMENTS OF COMMUNITY NETWORKS

You and the people you know offer more than connection. A connection catalyzes the existence of mutual value that can translate to professional assets. Some may think this sounds transactional. However, your community existed before this exchange and not because of it. Therefore, its sustainability is not based on this exchange but facilitated by your mutual desire to keep the relationship balanced.

CULTURAL COMPETENCE AS COMPETITIVE ADVANTAGE

Most of us have experienced the impact of assimilating into the dominant culture. We are probably aware of some of the nuances that come with the pressure or encouragement we face to assimilate in this environment. We need to make bold decisions about how we choose to leverage who we are, what we know, and what we are learning as a competitive advantage, rather than leaving these assets at the back door.

Modern Validation

Earlier in this chapter, we discussed the historical validation. Now, let us take a moment to discuss the modern validation, which comprises both evidence-based research and modern-day trends.

EVIDENCE-BASED RESEARCH

Statistical evidence of community leadership impact indicates that women with active community engagement show higher personal satisfaction in several areas. These areas are career trajectory, work satisfaction, team effectiveness, personal self-esteem, and leadership confidence.

The research shows that community involvement provided superior relationship-building skills compared to traditional professional networking.[82] By this, we mean that women who maintained strong community connections demonstrated more effective authentic relationship development and sustained professional influence.

Lastly, yet most surprisingly, women with significant family and community responsibilities showed higher levels of internal visibility activities and advocacy effectiveness. This contradicts widespread assumptions that community involvement limits professional advancement.

TRENDS

Some current business trends also validate the community being a leadership incubator. These trends include community-organizing principles as a corporate strategy, faith-based leadership in professional settings, and cultural networking.

Community-organizing principles include grassroots engagement, coalition building, issue framing, and movement building. Grassroots engagement shows up in workplaces as employee engagement and change management. Coalition building is presented as cross-functional collaboration and partnership development. Brand messaging and stakeholder communications are corporate speak for

---

82 Jones, "Quantitative Study."

issue framing and narrative. Sustainable movement building translates into organizational cultural development.

Faith-based leadership in professional settings includes servant leadership, ethical decision-making, community care principles, and vision development. Servant leadership presents as team development and mentorship programs in corporate settings. Ethical decision-making shows up as corporate governance and shareholder responsibility. Community care principles translate into employee well-being and retention strategies. Long-term vision development shows up as strategic planning and legacy thinking or development.

Cultural networking includes community connections, cultural authenticity, values alignment, and collective success models. Community connections translate into business development and market access. Cultural authenticity translates into brand credibility and customer loyalty. Values alignment translates to purpose-driven leadership and authentic engagement. Collective success models translate to team performance and organizational effectiveness.

Strategic Implementation

Strategic implementation is all about the high-level perspective you wish to take and your overall intentions or plan. It involves positioning, leveraging authenticity, and overcoming biases.

Positioning is all about language translation. That is, how you convert community roles into professional competencies. To successfully position yourself, you must document your achievements and translate the community impact into business or leadership terms. This is vital to reframing a narrative.

Leveraging authenticity is about integrating rather than code-switching. If you leverage your authenticity, you don't have to be someone else. You get to bring your full self and not leave part of yourself behind or switch part of yourself off. This is a key component of authentic leadership. Corporate settings that actively support authenticity create inclusive environments for others and conduct bridge building. When organizations leverage authenticity, they also give way to the effective modeling of revolutionary leadership. The best way to demonstrate revolutionary leadership is to model it in the workplace with pride and confidence.

Lastly, overcoming any professional bias against community experience is required in strategy implementation. These are professional biases that we have of ourselves, and the best way to overcome them is to use our results.

KEY TAKEAWAYS

- Community involvement is executive training, not volunteer work.
- Cultural networks are strategic professional assets.
- Translation is more important than transformation.
- Integration creates authentic authority.
- Community-developed approaches often outperform traditional methods.
- Community experience leads to better performance in crises, according to research.

ACTION STEPS

- List the leadership skills you have developed through church, community, or cultural organizations and that you've never thought to put on your resume. Rank your top five in terms of relevance to the types of jobs or consultancy roles that you apply for.
- Consider the life of your favorite Revolutionary Pathmaker. List at least three factors in her early life and community that contributed to or shaped her into the leader she became.

PART 2

Strategic Power

CHAPTER 6

Revolutionary Relationship Mastery

Success isn't just about what you know but who you lift up along the way. True mastery is in creating connections that inspire growth.
MICHELLE OBAMA

In part one, we focused on understanding the landscape of revolutionary leadership. Now, we shift our focus to understanding *strategic power* and how we can harness it as Revolutionary Pathmakers. We will begin by exploring *revolutionary relationship mastery/science*, which is a key aspect of strategic power. Black women have developed sophisticated, evidence-based relationship strategies that challenge traditional networking models. Their relationship-building approaches aren't just different from traditional networking; they're scientifically proven to be more effective.

It is worth noting that revolutionary relationship science isn't a marketing language. It is a precise description of what Black women have developed out of necessity and perfected through generations of practice.

CASE STUDY: THREE STROKES TO MIDNIGHT

The people who help you most are the ones who knew you before you needed help.
ROSALIND BREWER

One night, out of the blue, I got a call. It was Juanita. Juanita was a successful Black woman CEO. She was just fifteen months into her role at a midsize financial services company and happened to be their first Black woman leader.

The firm had recently hired two other Black women on the leadership team. Both Black women needed to be let go; one for embezzlement, the other for performance issues. As Juanita was instrumental in the hiring process, the company board questioned her hiring judgment. When the media caught wind of this story, the frenzy did not help. Understandably, Juanita started questioning her own leadership capacity.

Should I resign? *she wondered.*

Thankfully, she was willing to take on the different perspective I offered her. We worked with revolutionary insight to reframe the situation from "damage control" to "relationship leverage." Juanita had on her side fifteen years of built relationships as the foundation for her role as a "turning crisis into transformation" catalyst. And this was a better time than any to leverage this advantage.

Juanita swiftly put several resolutions into action. She began by holding transparent town halls and other company meetings.

Then she positioned the crisis as motivation for systemic change. This allowed her to launch new leadership development initiatives. Through her efforts, not only did she save her reputation, but she also turned this disastrous experience into an enriching one for the whole company. Our efforts were further validated when she received the "CEO of the Year" award, and the company became "number one for diversity, equity, and inclusion" (DEI). If that was not enough, Juanita was also appointed to a national leadership council.

POWER ACTIVATION PROMPT

Who has such deep knowledge of your character and capabilities that they could help you see possibilities instead of just problems?

Historical Context

The following are several examples of Black women who exercised revolutionary relationship mastery.

THE UNDERGROUND RAILROAD NETWORK

During enslavement, Black women, such as Harriet Tubman, created communication systems that saved lives. The Underground Railroad wasn't just about safe houses. It was about a relationship network that spanned hundreds of miles, built on trust that had to be absolute. One broken connection meant death. These women understood something that modern activists still struggle with: Information is only as powerful as the relationships that carry it. They didn't just pass messages. They built human infrastructure that could withstand surveillance, betrayal, and violence. To ensure a robust system, Tubman built redundancy into it. When one connection failed, three others could step in.[83] Harriet Tubman wasn't just brave; she was a master network architect. Her railroad worked because she understood relationship mapping at a level that would impress today's data scientists.

CHURCH AS A REVOLUTIONARY TRAINING GROUND

Black churches were not just spiritual centers. They were leadership academies disguised as Sunday service. Women who could not vote or hold public office ran complex church organizations with budgets, strategic planning, and political influence. Consider the Black women who led the Montgomery bus boycott in 1955.[84] They did not suddenly discover organizational skills; rather, they had been practicing those skills for decades in church committees, women's auxiliaries, and community groups. When Rosa Parks got arrested, these women's built-up power activated.

KITCHEN TABLE NETWORKS

Women who worked in white households during the day shared information that shaped movements, such as the Civil Rights Movement in the USA. Black women developed sophisticated information-sharing networks that operated below the radar of official surveillance. They understood family dynamics in powerful households. They under-

---

83 Shay Dawson, "Harriet Tubman," National Women's History Museum, 2024, https://www.womenshistory.org/education-resources/biographies/harriet-tubman.

84 "Montgomery Bus Boycott," The Martin Luther King, Jr. Research and Education Institute, accessed January 13, 2026, https://kinginstitute.stanford.edu/encyclopedia/montgomery-bus-boycott.

stood that real power often lived in spaces that looked powerless.[85] Take Fannie Lou Hamer, who was a powerful leader in the voting rights movement. Initially, her power didn't come from an official political position. It came from her relationships with sharecroppers, domestic workers, churchwomen, and other members of this Southern community, all of whom trusted her to speak truth on their behalf. When Hamer challenged the Democratic Party's efforts to block Black participation in 1964, she was not speaking as an individual; she was representing networks of women who had been organizing in invisible spaces for decades.[86]

ECONOMICS OF REVOLUTIONARY RELATIONSHIPS

Black women understood that protest without economic power was just performance. They built networks that could shift money, withdraw labor, and create alternative economic systems. During the Civil Rights Movement, women organized boycotts that worked because they controlled the household spending decisions. They knew which businesses depended on a Black customer base. They built relationships that could sustain economic pressure for months or even years. But they also created alternatives for when segregated stores would not serve them. When banks would not lend to them, they created information credit systems through churches and community groups. They understood that building up alternatives required breaking down barriers. The women who organized the Montgom-

85 Sylvia Marshall, "Nourishing the Movement: Georgia Gilmore's Club from Nowhere During the Montgomery Bus Boycott, 1955–1956" (master's thesis, University of North Carolina at Charlotte, 2022), https://ninercommons.charlotte.edu/record/1945/files/Marshall_uncc_0694N_13112.pdf.

86 "Fannie Lou Hamer," National Women's History Museum, accessed September 17, 2025. https://www.womenshistory.org/education-resources/biographies/fannie-lou-hamer.

ery bus boycott did not just stop riding buses; they created an entire transportation system using a network of car owners, churches with parking lots, and community volunteers. They turned relationship power into practical infrastructure.[87]

Research Validation

In general, the research[88] reveals insights that challenge every assumption about how power actually works. Black women's relationship structures are more sophisticated and effective than traditional models. Typically, they have been invisible to mainstream analysis because they do not look the way we expect power to look. Let us look deeper at what the research[89] tells us.

MULTI-HUB NETWORK MODEL

Black women's relationship systems do not mirror traditional, hierarchical networking structures that center a single senior sponsor or dominant gatekeeper. Across both time frames of my study, many women described and operated within what can best be understood as *multi-hub networks*: interconnected ecosystems of support, accountability, and influence distributed across different spaces in their lives.[90]

Rather than relying on one powerful mentor or executive ally, these women engaged in what I describe as *distributed sponsorship*, with different people advocating for them across different contexts. They had a colleague who affirmed their leadership capacity in team settings, a senior leader who supported their advancement in organi-

87 Ibid.

88 Jones, "Quantitative Study."

89 Ibid.

90 Ibid.

zational spaces, a community elder or peer who provided grounding and guidance, and a professional contact who amplified their expertise in external environments.

This structure did not eliminate vulnerability, but it reduced dependency on any single relationship, gatekeeper, or institution. In periods of organizational volatility or change, these multi-hub networks provided continuity, perspective, and stability—not because they guaranteed upward mobility, but because they created relational anchors across otherwise fragile systems.

This is not an alternative version of traditional networking. It is a fundamentally different relational logic—one rooted in collective resilience rather than individual gatekeeping.

AUTHENTICITY ADVANTAGE

My research also challenges the assumption that authenticity is a liability for Black women in professional spaces.[91] Across interviews and narrative responses, women who have remained connected to their communities, values, and cultural identities did not describe authenticity as the opposite of professionalism—they described it as a source of grounding and coherence.

However, authenticity was most sustainable when it was supported by strong relationship networks. Women who attempted to assimilate entirely—suppressing aspects of their identity to fit the dominant norms—often reported increased exhaustion, disconnection, and diminished well-being, even when they appeared externally successful. By contrast, women whose relationships expanded beyond the workplace and who maintained ties to community leadership, faith networks, or social collectives had greater access to emotional support, strategic guidance, and perspective.

91 Jones, "Quantitative Study."

These women's community-rooted leadership did not merely mirror traditional executive models; it broadened them. The skills women cultivated through community roles—conflict navigation, resource stewardship, intergenerational care, and coalition building—informed how they led inside organizations and entrepreneurial spaces. Rather than adapting themselves to existing leadership frames, many women expanded the very meaning of leadership in the environments they occupied.[92]

INFORMATION VELOCITY FACTOR

One of the most striking relational patterns in my research relates to how information circulates within Black women's networks.[93] [94] Rather than following primarily through formal reporting lines or hierarchical channels, information in these networks often moved through trust-based, multidirectional relationships.

This produced what I describe as *information velocity*: not simply the speed of information, but the ability to detect emerging change earlier and interpret it through meaningful relational contexts. Women frequently became aware of organizational shifts, leadership transitions, or economic disruptions before they were formally announced; not because they had privileged institutional access, but because their relationships operated across multiple spheres at once—professional, communal, spiritual, and social.

This anticipatory awareness did not always translate into protection or advantage. Instead, it often allowed women to prepare emotionally, strategically, and relationally for instability—to steady themselves, support others, and adapt with greater clarity. In this

92 Brown, "Revolutionary Evidence."

93 Jones, "Quantitative Study."

94 Ibid.

sense, information velocity became less about competitive positioning and more about survival navigation in unpredictable systems.[95]

COLLECTIVE SUCCESS MODEL

Perhaps the most significant insight across the research challenges widely held narratives of individual achievement.[96] The women in these studies did not describe success as an isolated personal ascent. Instead, they framed success as deeply relational—emerging through shared support, mutual investment, and collective accountability.

Lifting others as they advanced was not simply an ethical stance; it was a form of stability building. Collective success strengthened relational trust, generated shared knowledge resources, and created networks capable of absorbing disruption in ways that purely individual strategies could not. This was not charity. It was strategic, community-centered leadership praxis.

Rather than competing for scarce opportunity, many women built ecosystems in which opportunity could circulate. This mode of leadership affirms something Black women have long known: Thriving alone is neither sustainable nor liberatory—thriving together can produce forms of power that endure beyond any one role, organization, or moment in time.[97]

Power Dynamics/Analysis

The reality is that the power Black women possess often does not resemble the power other groups have. To understand this, we need

95 Ibid.

96 Ibid.

97 Ibid.

to look at power in terms of what works and what does not, through historical and modern lenses.

HISTORICAL POWER PATTERNS/INVISIBLE INFRASTRUCTURE

In the past, Black women's power operated through what we can consider *invisible infrastructure systems.* These systems created real change while appealing to existing hierarchies. During Jim Crow, Black women teachers had no official political power, but they shaped entire generations of leaders through classroom relationships. They could not run for office, but they determined who got educated. Many could not vote, but they influenced how educated Black communities understood their rights and possibilities.

American educator Septima Poinsette Clark's educational programs were not just about literacy. They were about building political infrastructure through educational relationships. Clark understood that teaching people to read was teaching them to challenge power. She built networks of teachers who could replicate her model across the South. When the Civil Rights Movement needed to be educated by politically conscious participants, her relationship networks provided them.[98]

CONTEMPORARY POWER TRANSLATION

Black women are still building power through relationships that look educational, supportive, or service oriented but which create structural changes. The most effective Black women leaders in the workforce are not just advancing their own careers. They are changing organizational cultures through relationship building. They are creating

98 "Clark, Septima Poinsette," The Martin Luther King, Jr. Research and Education Institute, accessed January 14, 2026, https://kinginstitute.stanford.edu/clark-septima-poinsette.

inclusive environments by building coalitions. They are shifting power dynamics by developing other leaders.[99] My 2025[100] data shows that Black women in the highest leadership roles who maintain community connections are more likely to implement successful inclusion initiatives. Their community relationships give them credibility, perspective, and networks that support organizational change work.

CODE-SWITCHING POWER ANALYSIS

Black women operate in multiple power systems simultaneously. The research reveals how successful women navigate these systems without losing effectiveness in any of them. Code-switching is not just about language or behavior. It is about relationship management across different power structures. The most successful women in the study maintained authentic relationships in multiple contexts while strategically adapting their approach to maximize their influence in each setting.[101]

RESISTANCE AND NAVIGATION FRAMEWORK

Black women's power exists in constant tension with systems designed to exclude them. The research shows how successful navigation requires both distance and accommodation strategies deployed through relationship networks. Effective Black women leaders use relationships to create alternatives. They build enough institutional power to change systems from within while maintaining the external relationships needed to survive should institutional power fail, as it often does. My research data shows that women with strong boundary-spanning relationships, connections that cross racial, organizational, and social

99 Jones, "Quantitative Study."

100 Brown, "Revolutionary Evidence."

101 Ibid.

boundaries, have higher success rates in terms of both advancement and impact. They can operate effectively in white-dominated spaces while maintaining authentic connections to Black communities.[102]

Success Patterns

My research and other studies reveal that approaches dismissed as soft or alternative are actually more effective than traditional models. But only when they are supported by strong relationship infrastructure and strategic implementation. Now, let us look at each relevant success pattern.

COLLABORATIVE LEADERSHIP ADVANTAGE

Traditional leadership theory emphasizes individual decision-making and hierarchical control. Black women's leadership approaches emphasize collective intelligence and distributed power. The research shows which approach works better.[103] Data supports that organizations led by Black women show higher employee engagement scores and better problem-solving outcomes on complex challenges.[104] These women are accessing collective intelligence that individual leaders cannot match. The data reveals why: Complex organizational challenges require diverse perspectives and buy-in from multiple stakeholders. Leaders who can build connections, facilitate conversations, and integrate different viewpoints are more effective than those who rely on positional authority.

---

102 Ibid.

103 Jones, "Quantitative Study."

104 Ajhanai Channel Inez Keaton, "Black Women Diversity Leaders' Perceptions of Organizational Inclusivity in College Sports," *Frontiers in Sports and Active Living* 4 (2022): 923649, https://doi.org/10.3389/fspor.2022.923649.

EMOTIONAL INTELLIGENCE IMPACT

Black women's leadership approaches integrate emotional intelligence, which traditional models do not consider an important aspect of "real" leadership. My research shows that this integration is a competitive advantage. Leadership that marries strategic thinking and emotional awareness has higher success in managing organizational change and better outcomes in managing through crisis.[105] This is because such leaders can read organizational dynamics, anticipate resistance, and build support for difficult decisions. This is not just about individual emotional intelligence. It is about relationship-based emotional intelligence.

VALUES-BASED AUTHORITY MODEL

Black women often lead from values rather than position. The research shows this creates more sustainable authority than traditional power-based models. Leaders who can articulate clear values, demonstrate consistency in their actions, and build teams around shared purpose have higher retention rates and better performance on long-term goals.[106] This validates something Black women have learned through necessity: When you cannot rely on positional power, you must build moral authority. When systems do not automatically respect you, you must earn respect through demonstration. When traditional influence channels are closed, you must create influence through relationship and values alignment.

105 Ibid.

106 Jones, "Quantitative Study."

COMMUNITY INTEGRATION SUCCESS FACTORS

Another significant research finding challenges the separation between professional and community leadership. The research shows that Black women who maintain strong community connections are more effective in professional leadership. Women with active community involvement show higher leadership effectiveness ratings and better outcomes on team-building and organizational culture initiatives. Their communication experiences give them skills that cannot be learned in corporate training programs. Community leadership requires managing volunteers, building consensus without authority, creating vision that inspires action, and navigating complex relationship dynamics. These skills translate directly to professional effectiveness, but they are developed outside traditional professional development systems.[107]

LONG-TERM RELATIONSHIP INVESTMENT PATTERN

Black women's leadership approaches emphasize long-term building over short-term transactional gains. The research shows this creates sustainable power that weathers organizational changes. Leaders who invest in long-term relationships have higher survival rates during organizational restrictions and better outcomes when transitioning to new roles. Their relationship capital transfers across contexts in ways that positional power cannot.[108] The research shows this is not just morally superior. It is strategically smarter.[109]

These success patterns reveal that Black women have not been using alternative leadership approaches. They have been using advanced leadership approaches that mainstream models are finally catching up to.

---

107 Ibid.

108 Ibid.

109 Ibid.

KEY TAKEAWAYS

- Networking to relationship science: Stop thinking about building connections, and start thinking about creating systems.
- Assimilation to translation: Stop trying to network like others, and start teaching others to build relationships like you.
- Individual to ecosystem: Your advancement is not separate from your community's advancement.
- Deficit to asset: Your community connections, cultural competencies, and relationship approaches are professional assets, not personal quirks.

ACTION STEPS

Pick at least one action step to execute today:

- Review your relationship portfolio, and identify one area that needs attention.
- Find one way to share your community leadership experience in a professional context.
- Make one ask that feels natural and mutual.

CHAPTER 7

Beyond White Male Networking Models

I am a Black woman, and I will not be limited by anyone's expectations but my own. My ambition is my rebellion against a world that tries to define me.

OPRAH WINFREY

As we know, white male networking models don't work for Black women or, at best, are not as effective. Therefore, we need to learn about what does and what doesn't work. In this chapter, we will focus our attention on networking models that are conducive to Black women's thriving.

CASE STUDY: JUST BE YOU!

Always bring your whole self to the table, including your personality, your sense of humor, and your experience.

MELLODY HOBSON

You are killing it! You are a Black woman in a senior public relations role at a tech startup. Not only that, but you have over a decade of work experience and recently completed an MBA program. You were promoted to this role and are seeking to build your industry influence and executive presence. With that desire, you went and got yourself some advice from a high-profile executive coach who had been working with the firm. This man, who happens to be white, recommends aggressive LinkedIn networking. Can you picture it?

Well, this is exactly the situation that Lucy found herself in. Her coach's advice was for her to invest $5,000 in a personal branding consultant, professional photos, and a LinkedIn Premium subscription. His strategy for her was for her to connect with at least fifty industry leaders weekly, engage with all their content, and position herself as a thought leader.

Well, she did it.

It was a disaster.

During the first three months of aggressively following the coach's LinkedIn outreach templates, Lucy did not stray from the plan. She commented on posts with generic business insights and sent connection requests to white male executives she had never met. For two hours a day, she managed a LinkedIn persona that felt completely artificial, because it was. It was very draining for her. However, that was not the worst of it.

The whole plan went downhill and backfired. There was an industry controversy involving the disproportionate impact of AI data centers on Black communities. Her generic engagement strategy put her on the wrong side of an important issue. Fur-

thermore, community members saw her LinkedIn activity and questioned the alignment of her values. She lost credibility with both her corporate network and her community base.

Thankfully, all was not lost. When she sought my assistance, we identified a solution. Her revolutionary pivot was the realization that her most valuable professional connections came from completely different sources.

LinkedIn strategy results, in her case, generated zero meaningful professional opportunities and damaged her community relationships. Thankfully, repairing and then prioritizing those affected community relationships resulted in a $175,000 client contract, a board position, and authentic professional relationships. Traditional networking advice created professional damage, while authentic community connections generated career advancement.

POWER ACTIVATION PROMPT

What if incongruous and exhausting networking advice is keeping you from leveraging the relationship strengths that actually work?

Architect of Exclusion

To dismantle the methodology of biased universal networking advice, we need to understand why traditional networking fails, confront the assumptions that create exclusion, and address performance sustainability problems.

WHY TRADITIONAL NETWORKING ADVICE FAILS BLACK WOMEN

The main reason traditional networking advice is inadequate for Black women is simple: access. Traditional networking advice assumes that there is universal access to participate or engage with a network, with none of the same barriers to entry. Unfortunately, that is not the case. Of course, there are times when Black women gain access, but they are cultural outsiders in those spaces, and they end up paying a premium price, including endless code-switching and emotional labor and the suppression of authenticity.

THE ASSUMPTIONS

Assumptions around culture, economics, and society are embedded in networking approaches, including the traditional networking model. One such assumption in the traditional networking model is that you must assimilate. Cultural assimilation is a trap. It demands that you fit into the company culture if you want professional advancement.

This assumes that the culture is neutral, rather than reflecting the preferences of those with the most power. It supposes that we build our rapport through shared interests and that those interests are shared across cultural differences. Common shared interests among traditionally powerful groups typically include sports such as golf, pickleball, or tennis and lifestyle habits such as social drinking. To fit in, you must maintain different versions of yourself, which becomes exhausting. This is a demand for assimilation that's backed up by the threat of fragility when we are unable to assimilate.

Another widespread assumption is that of individual achievement. This is a delusion that favors competition over contribution or reciprocity. White male networking models focus on extraction. Connect with someone powerful, extract what you need, and move on. Black women practice mutual value creation. They think about what both people gain. This comes from understanding that individual success means little if your community remains excluded. Black women rarely advance alone. They need collective strength because systems work against them individually.

PERFORMANCE SUSTAINABILITY CHALLENGES

Relationships built on cultural performances require constant performance. Not only does this lead us to burn out, but it also does not lend itself to higher job satisfaction because we are not able to be our authentic selves.[110]

Research Insights

Across both time frames of my research,[111] it became clear that traditional—and largely white male—networking models are built on assumptions that do not reflect the lived conditions of Black women's leadership. These models presuppose uninterrupted availability, low caregiving responsibility, access to socially exclusive environments, and the protection of institutional power. They reward visibility that is publicly performative but not relationally accountable.

Black women do not enter leadership from within those conditions.

Rather than simply believing they failed to adapt to dominant networking models, many women in the research described experiencing these structures as misaligned—socially inaccessible, emotionally extractive, or strategically unproductive. What is often interpreted as networking avoidance is, in many cases, a form of discernment.

110 Keaton, "Organizational Inclusivity."

111 Jones, "Quantitative Study."

In 2010,[112] women who sustained meaningful community and cultural relationships did not merely report stronger satisfaction—they described those relationships as grounding, protective, and clarifying. Community networks provided perspective, identity coherence, and reciprocal support that corporate networking spaces rarely offered. These networks helped women navigate conflict, interpret organizational dynamics, and remain connected to values that shaped their leadership purpose.

My 2025[113] analysis deepens this understanding. Networking among Black women—particularly in the years following COVID-19—frequently functions as stabilization and recovery work rather than as opportunistic advancement. Women increase relationship engagement not to gain a competitive edge but to maintain continuity, share resources, and steady themselves and others through periods of uncertainty. Relational labor, in this context, is not ancillary to leadership—it is a survival infrastructure.

This stands in sharp contrast to traditional networking logics, which are designed to consolidate advantage rather than distribute support. Where dominant models privilege individual status accumulation, Black women's networks, by necessity, operate as ecosystems of mutual reliance, shared responsibility, and care.

The research does not suggest that Black women benefit less from opportunity-bearing relationships. Rather, it reveals that the structures most celebrated in mainstream narratives of professional networking are often incompatible with the social, relational, and caregiving realities Black women are expected to carry. Their leadership thrives in relational systems that recognize interdependence—not in environments that reward isolation and hierarchy.

---

112 Ibid.

113 Brown, "Revolutionary Evidence."

Construct Evidence-Based Alternatives

These are strategies that honor community-based approaches and include a professional community care model and cultural intelligence advantage. The apparatus that makes this approach successful is the transformation of existing community relationships into professional advancement opportunities through systemic value creation and strategic positioning. Such positioning is for the greater good, not just for individual gain.

PROFESSIONAL COMMUNITY CARE MODEL

Moving away from white male networking models and deliberately including care efforts addresses community challenges as professional skills breed success. These care efforts can include business mentoring, leadership training, financial literacy workshops, and much more.

CULTURAL INTELLIGENCE ADVANTAGE

Alongside the professional community care model, the cultural intelligence advantage factors into the construction of evidence-based alternatives to white male networking models. With a cultural intelligence advantage, you can position multicultural competency as consulting value for organizations seeking diverse market access. You can use cultural insights to identify market opportunities and demographic trends before they appear in formal research. At the same time, you get to leverage cultural connections to facilitate business relationships across different communities.

KEY TAKEAWAYS

- Stop trying to build connections. Start creating systems of mutual value that compound over time.
- Your cultural identity and community experience are professional assets and not liabilities to overcome.
- Your advancement and your community's advancement are interconnected and not competing priorities.
- Instead of seeking entry into existing networks, create networks others want to join.

ACTION STEPS

Pick at least one action step to complete:

- Document specific examples of professional value creation through cultural authenticity or community connections.
- Build a reputation as a connector who helps others access opportunities and insights they couldn't reach independently.

CHAPTER 8

Revolutionary Visibility

Never be limited by other people's limited imaginations; never limit others because of your own limited imagination.

DR. MAE JEMISON

In this chapter, we will address the topic of visibility and how you can ensure not only that you are seen in every room you step into but also that your contributions are fully appreciated. First, let's define two important terms we will use throughout this chapter: internal visibility and strategic presence.

Internal visibility is when you are seen by decision-makers as doing meaningful work. *Strategic presence* is when you are memorable and respected without exhausting yourself. Rather than feeling like you must be physically present everywhere, strategic presence is about being impactful where it matters.

POWER ACTIVATION PROMPT

When was the last time you spoke up in a meeting? Did you measure your words? Calculate the risk? Wonder if you'd be seen as too much or not enough? The mental math is the tax Black women pay for visibility. This chapter is about reducing that tax while increasing your impact.

CASE STUDY: CONFERENCE ROOM CALCULATION

I didn't learn to be quiet when I had an opinion. The reason they knew who I was is because I told them.
URSULA BURNS

I was in my early thirties, and I was steadily climbing the career ladder. At the time, I was one of only two Black women in a finance division of two hundred staff in an exceptionally profitable enterprise. On one occasion, I was invited to a strategic planning meeting—the kind of meeting where you are being evaluated. With that understanding, I spent a full weekend preparing. I wanted to ensure my contribution to the discussion would be worth every second.

On the day of the meeting, my moment arrived to contribute my insights. I had an answer ready, but they said, "Let's hear from somebody else … Tim." This was odd to me because Tim was not working on anything related to the topic, but I certainly was. On top of that, Tim had the floor for ten minutes.

I was determined to leave a mark, so I attempted to speak again. And I was interrupted again. However, this time, I decided not to stand for it. I paused. Then I said, "To complete my point ..." and continued until I had fully articulated my recommendations.

The expressions on some of the other attendees' faces said it all. What? Did she just keep going?! *But that didn't matter to me. What did matter was the immediate feedback I obtained from the senior vice president: "Good points, Kerry. Let's explore them."*

A few moments later, leadership adopted two of my recommendations.

Of course, I was delighted that they saw value in what I shared, but I was also exhausted. After this meeting, I reflected on the full experience.

There had to be a more energy-efficient and self-honoring way to make my value undeniable. I was done with having to communicatively wrestle for a spotlight in these meetings, done trying to prove my worth to participants who were primed not to see me or the value I had to offer.

Ultimately, I realized that I didn't have to wait until I got into those rooms to attain visibility. I stopped trying to prove I deserved to be in every room, and instead, I began to choose the rooms that deserved my presence. This gave me immediate efficiency gains. In addition, I began to track and document my return on investment (ROI) on aspects of the business that I felt were important, data that I then presented back to leadership. This data included what I had accomplished the previous month, my current performance, and my targets for the following month. It was a simple matter of sharing regular updates about the ROI on my portfolio with leadership.

Several months later, I was promoted. The numbers in my ROI portfolio spoke for themselves. I am certain that attending and fighting to be heard in all the meetings I was invited to would not have led to the same outcome.

The Visibility Paradox

To get the results I achieved in the previous case study, you must ask yourself, "Am I being seen by the right people?" If you aren't, how can you make sure you are seen by the right people, for the right things? That is the *visibility paradox*. It's not about being seen. It is about being seen for the right things and by the right or most relevant decision-makers. This is an important challenge to solve because you cannot advance without visibility.

Visibility in corporate meetings or other scenarios may work for others. You must assess if the energy and effort you are putting in justifies the payoff. As Black women, we need to think about energy management when we talk about the visibility paradox.

Historical Context

We met a host of Black women in previous chapters who have achieved visibility, Black women such as Ursula Burns, Angela Davis, Shirley Chisholm, Audre Lorde, Winnie Mandela, Ellen Johnson Sirleaf, and many others. But the reality is that most Black women who were Revolutionary Pathmakers did not make it to the history books—not because they did not make significant contributions to their communities and beyond, but because they were not valued by those who get to write history. This is emblematic of the sheer magnitude of the systemic bias they battled.

Post-1940, there was a rapid integration of Black women into the workforce. Historically, Black women in the labor force far outnumbered white women, but this gap closed as the number of white women in the workforce increased significantly. This shift was shaped by multiple converging forces—including wartime labor demands, changes in industrial employment, economic restructuring, educational expansion, and evolving gender norms—alongside rising household financial requirements. Increased wages played a role, but so did the broader social, political, and economic pressure that reshaped how women across racial groups participated in work.[114]

As Black women integrated into the workforce, they had to be both excellent—but not too excellent—and nonthreatening to the status quo. Therefore, they had to assimilate. These Black women worked as if the outcomes of anyone else being there didn't change anything. If they had bold ideas, they had to frame them as a question, lest they appear too ambitious and too uppity. With that ethos, Black women worked in these spaces through the sixties and seventies, making it better for those who came in the eighties and nineties. And they learned to be visible in ways that built influence without provoking backlash.

114 Leah Platt Boustan and William J. Collins, "The Origins and Persistence of Black-White Differences in Women's Labor Force Participation," Working Paper No. 19040 (National Bureau of Economic Research, May 2013), http://doi.org/10.3386/w19040.

Research Validation

Across both my 2010[115] and 2025[116] studies, internal visibility consistently emerged as a meaningful factor in Black women's leadership trajectories, but in ways far more complex than traditional leadership narratives suggest. Internal visibility matters, yet the experience of being visible is shaped by structural expectations, relational burden, and the emotional labor of managing perception.

In the earlier study, activities that increased internal visibility, such as leading high-exposure projects, serving on strategic committees, and building relationships with key decision-makers, were associated with higher promotion trajectories over time. However, even within those outcomes, many women described carrying a double burden: performing the work itself while also ensuring the work was seen, understood, and legitimized by others.

By contrast, external visibility, speaking at conferences, publishing articles, or serving on external boards did not consistently correlate with organizational advancement. These activities enhanced reputation and credibility, but they did not always translate into internal opportunities. For many women, external recognition coexisted with internal invisibility.

My 2025 research[117] deepens and complicates this story. In remote, hybrid, and matrixed environments, internal visibility has become both more necessary and more difficult to sustain. Without informal encounters or shared physical spaces, visibility requires intentional relationship building, continuous communication across multiple reporting lines, and persistent emotional effort. Black women described navigating expanded spheres of accountability—influenc-

115 Jones, "Quantitative Study."

116 Brown, "Revolutionary Evidence."

117 Brown, "Revolutionary Evidence."

ing supervisors, collaborators, and dispersed stakeholders—while also guarding against misinterpretation or erasure.

At the same time, increased visibility did not always produce a greater sense of opportunity, safety, or authority. For some women, visibility heightened their exposure to scrutiny, performance pressure, and representational burden. The work of remaining visible and managing how they were perceived frequently existed alongside the caregiving responsibilities, community commitments, and relational labor they already carried outside the workplace.

Across both studies, a persistent tension appeared: the expectation that Black women be both highly competent and relationally agreeable while rarely being permitted to inhibit both identities without consequence. Many women described the mental load of constantly calibrating tone, presence, and expression to ensure their contributions were recognized without being mischaracterized.

The research does not suggest that visibility should be avoided but reveals that visibility is not simply about being seen; it is about navigating systems that require Black women to demonstrate value while simultaneously moderating how that value is allowed to appear.[118] Revolutionary visibility, then, is not about showing up everywhere. It is about investing presence where it matters, preserving energy, and insisting on visibility without self-erasure.

Strategic Presence: A Framework

It remains true that the organizations that advance Black women are those where Black women can be visible without exhaustion, valuable without performativity, and powerful without compromise. In essence, that is what revolutionary visibility is. It is the strategic

118 Ibid.

approach to professional presence that moves beyond proving that you deserve to be in the room to choosing the rooms that deserve your presence. It's not about being the loudest but about being the voice people respect.

The Strategic Presence Framework helps you master presence using specific tactics that are readily available.

FOUR-PART STRATEGIC PRESENCE FRAMEWORK WITH TACTICS

1. **Know your value position:** Be aware of what you bring that others don't. Know the problems you solve. Understand the perspective you offer. Write all these down, and look for opportunities to demonstrate them.
2. **Choose your moments:** You don't need to speak up at every meeting. You just need to speak up in the right meetings, at the right time. When you want to speak up, ask yourself if this is your area of expertise. Will your perspective add something that others have not yet contributed? Is the decision-maker even listening?
3. **Make your work visible before it's done:** Share easy wins, ask for input at key points, and give others credit for their input. Don't wait until the final presentation to let people know about your project—instead, bring them along on your journey. If you're bringing others in, it is not just your project anymore. These contributors have become stakeholders, allowing you to build champions for your work before you need them.
4. **Create visibility systems:** Do not simply rely on people noticing your good work; create systems to make it visible.

This might mean making regular updates within your reporting structure, sharing quick wins in team meetings, and documenting impact. Keep in mind that outcomes that are measured really matter. Revolutionary Pathmakers know that it is not enough to do good work; the right people must know about it. One word of caution: If you don't create these visibility systems, people will fill the unknown with whatever they want, and if you are not measuring your outcomes, you may not be able to convincingly dispute the story they formulate.

Strategic Presence Without Performativity

We have all heard the adage, "Just be yourself!" For Black women, this advice is incomplete. Yes, studies[119] show that leaders who can be authentic are effective and less exhausted. But there's a trap: Authenticity for Black women in white spaces comes at a cost. Authenticity isn't about showing every part of yourself, in every context, and exercising full transparency. It is about never having to completely hide who you are; it's about finding that balance. You can be strategic about what you share and when while still being true to yourself. It's not fake; it's smart.

Strategic presence requires you to assess when to lean in versus when to take a more measured stance, especially in high-stakes situations. This is a vital calculation that you must make, particularly when there are people who are going to use that information against you. It is an even more important consideration when you are the

---

119 Judith Kampa et al., "Mechanisms Linking Authentic Leadership to Emotional Exhaustion: The Role of Procedural Justice and Emotional Demands in a Moderated Mediation Approach," *Industrial Health* 55, no. 2 (2016): 95–107, https://doi.org/10.2486/indhealth.2016-0046.

only Black woman in the room. Fundamentally, it's about strategic energy management.

To exercise revolutionary presence, you must redefine executive presence. You must do this because traditional executive presence was modeled after white male leadership. White male leadership norms value certain types of communication styles, ways of being, and presentations of power. Under such models, Black women are virtually powerless because all those things are outside our control. Further still, Black women often get feedback that we lack executive presence.

Revolutionary presence offers a better way, grounded in competence, not performance. Rooted in authenticity, not assimilation. Cast in influence, not domination. A way that is sustainable and not exhaustive.

To build your version of revolutionary presence, use the following four tactics:

1. **Know what your power source is:** It might be your relationship, perspective, or unique skill. Whatever it is, lean into it instead of trying to manufacture it. No "fake it till you make it," because Revolutionary Pathmakers are not performative.
2. **Develop your signature style:** Figure out your style for naturally commanding the room. You might do it, for example, through your sense of worth or your precision, or you might use storytelling or piles of data. Whatever your style is, find it and refine it. Don't copy someone else's style. If you copy something, it may not be your superpower. If you are not a good analyst, don't use heavy datasets as the core of your style. In my case, warmth and groundedness are the core of my signature style. Often, my presence has helped calm chaotic encounters.

3. **Practice strategic competence:** It's not about believing you are the best at everything. If you are clear about what you are good at and know your zone of competence, you don't need to perform confidence; you already have it. If you are not yet where you want to be, be honest about what you are still learning.

4. **Use structure to support yourself:** You don't have to reengineer everything. You can structure frameworks for tough conversations and even have templates for key communications. Practice how to ground yourself before high-stakes moments. Contrary to what some may think, structure isn't the opposite of authenticity. Structure allows you to be authentic under pressure.

Sustainable Visibility

Black women often believe that we must prove our value constantly. As a result, we overwork, over-deliver, and overextend ourselves. Because we must constantly make ourselves visible, this becomes a trap and a vicious cycle. Research shows that the women who are the most exhausted are not getting promoted as often.[120] These women are too busy proving their value to build the relationships that lead to advancement. They have not been investing in activities that give them a higher return on their efforts. This continuous attempt to remain visible comes at a heavy price for Black women. I refer to it as the *performativity tax.*

120 Jaclyn Margolis, "Overlooked Reasons Why Women Don't Get Promoted," *Psychology Today*, April 28, 2023, https://www.psychologytoday.com/us/blog/shifting-workplace-dynamics/202304/overlooked-reasons-why-women-dont-get-promoted.

PERFORMATIVITY TAX, OR THE EXHAUSTION PROBLEM

We don't say it enough: Visibility is exhausting for Black women in ways it isn't for others. You are managing your competence, visibility, authenticity, and impact, as well as the threat level, all at the same time. This is extra mental and emotional energy that you must spend managing perception while simply trying to handle your responsibilities. One sign of a high *performativity* tax is feeling exhausted after every meeting because you felt as though you were performing at all times. This performance takes more time than the actual work.

At this point, you may be wondering how to build visibility sustainably. Here's an approach that works for me.

Building Sustainable Visibility

This approach involves three tactics:

1. **Pick your platforms:** As we learned with strategic presence, we don't need to be everywhere. So, choose two to three platforms or mediums where your targeted audience pays focused attention and ensure that the audience knows who you are and what you are up to. Do not spread yourself too thin.

   If you are inside an organization, consider attending leadership meetings and planning sessions. If you are outside an organization, join and be active in one professional organization and on one social media platform.

2. **Conduct batch work:** Schedule or block out time specifically for visibility activities. Don't scatter it around. For example, select one day a week, fortnight, or month when you spend time doing internal relationship building or other visibility

activities. On other days, focus on deep work. This gives you recovery time.

3. **Track ROI:** Track the activities that lead to opportunities. Make sure your visibility, ROI, and energy spent combined make sense in terms of the opportunity and advancement gain. I encourage women to be ruthless about this because energy is finite. It is imperative that you find out where you send your energy and if it is worth the expense.

Demonstrating Value Without Exhausting Yourself

1. **Define the value:** Before you start a project, be clear about what success looks like. Document and get agreement. This way, when you deliver, you don't have to convince people of the value.
2. **Qualify what matters:** Find out the ways people measure or track objectives. For example, if it's reducing costs, numbers are hard to dismiss.
3. **Tell your impact story:** Don't bullet point your accomplishments. Explain your impact, and make your value undeniable.
4. **Build advocates:** Who else can tell this story? How do you create something that other people talk about? When someone else tells your story, it lands differently.

KEY TAKEAWAYS

- You don't need to be visible everywhere. You need to be unforgettable in the right places.
- You don't need to prove your value constantly. You need to demonstrate it strategically.
- You don't need to exhaust yourself performing. You need to show up powerfully, in ways that are sustainable.
- Revolutionary visibility isn't about being seen all the time. It is about being seen, heard, and remembered when it matters most. And it's about doing it without losing yourself in the process.

ACTION STEPS

- Identify your top three visibility opportunities.
- Have conversations with potential advocates about your goals, and note down key insights.

Explore the featured or additional resources on https://revolutionarylead.com/ for more help.

CHAPTER 9

Strategic Resource Leverage

Energy management is more important than time management. Protect your energy like your career depends on it, because it does.

THASUNDA BROWN DUCKETT

In the previous chapter, we discussed revolutionary visibility. In this chapter, we turn our attention to how you can effectively maneuver the allocation of resources to achieve maximum gains. You will learn how to leverage your resources strategically around a variety of assets. The goal of this chapter is to help you reclaim your resources and direct them strategically.

Here, we define *resources* and *assets* as your time (hours), energy (mental and emotional), attention, well-being (physical and mental), relationships, credibility (reputation), and, of course, money (what you can afford to invest).

CASE STUDY: FINALE

I did what my conscience told me to do,
and you can't fail if you do that.
ANITA HILL

The year I was finalizing my doctoral program, I had two teenagers, one in boarding school on the other side of the country and another preparing to enroll in a school in the South. During this time, I was also determining next steps regarding my career and personal life, which had been on hold. I was working full-time, flying cross-country for school visits and performances, writing and analyzing data nonstop, and trying to figure out what would come next.

Everyone said I was impressive. The reality was, I was just barely managing. My breaking point was looming. It came on one of the days with back-to-back meetings. On that day, I arrived at work at eight o'clock in the morning, after a night with less than four hours of sleep. I hadn't eaten. I hadn't checked in with my daughter, who had called in tears the night before.

When I stepped into my office, I closed the door and sat at my desk.

Then I cried.

Once I'd pulled it together, I made a spreadsheet. Listed everything I was doing and calculated the cost.

The math told me that 60 percent of my time was spent on activities that contributed to 10 percent of my actual goals. The question changed from "How do I fit more in?" to "What can I cut out?" Within six months, I had cut thirty hours of commitments weekly. I started getting enough sleep again. I had time to eat and enjoy my meals. Once again, I was present.

Finally, I finished my dissertation. My work performance improved. To top it off, I was even clearer about my next steps: I decided to leave the company I worked for.

The secret wasn't doing more; it was doing less of what didn't matter.

POWER ACTIVATION PROMPT

You've been told your whole life to work twice as hard. But what if the strategy isn't to work harder? What if it's working smarter by doing less of what doesn't matter and more of what does?

The Resource Reality

We know that resources are finite for everyone. However, Black women are under additional and unique resource constraints. These constraints are a result of systems and dynamics that request more from them. These factors that try to hold Black women often include invisible labor, such as participating in DEI committees, representing our communities, and undertaking work that is expected but rarely recognized and rewarded. At the same time, Black women are constructed in the public imagination as infinitely strong and not requiring support. To meet these expectations, we add on further work, such as code-switching.

Traditional advice to work twice as hard ignores the reality expressed above. It assumes that we are starting from the same baseline as everyone else. That is not the case. Fortunately, there are ways to overcome these limitations. One approach that I will share with you in this chapter is the *Strategic Allocation Framework*. Through this approach, you ensure that you do not work twice as hard. Rather, you recognize all the limitations and challenges and make strategic choices to give yourself the upper hand that you deserve.

Historical Innovation in Energy Conservation

In previous generations, Black women had unique ways of managing the energy needed to fulfill their roles. However, before we discuss these roles, it is vital that we understand that this is not about celebrating struggle. Rather, this is about recognizing that Black women have always known something that leadership literature is just learning: You succeed by doing the right thing strategically. And Black women have always been strategic across their roles, some of which are highlighted here.

Domestic work: Black women raised families while working in other people's homes. They managed multiple households, multiple sets of kids, and multiple demands on limited time. These women became masters at doing what was essential and letting go of the rest.

Church leadership: Black women led congregations, organized communities, and provided spiritual guidance. They achieved all this while also working full-time jobs and raising their own families. They learned to maximize impact through strategic delegation and by building systems that worked without them.

The Civil Rights Movement: Black women organized boycotts and registered voters; they built the Civil Rights Movement while holding down their own jobs and managing their own homes. They didn't do everything; they did the things that mattered. Then they mobilized others to do the rest.

Corporate pioneers: Being "the first" of anything often comes with its own challenges. It was no different for the first Black women in white-collar spaces, navigating hostile environments. They quickly learned which battles to fight and when to save their energy. All the while, they also mentored the next generation of Black women.

Single mothers: Many Black women built careers while raising children alone. Often, they had to make impossible choices daily as they navigated where to invest their limited resources.

The Strategic Allocation Framework

To overcome all these pressures, you need an effective approach. The Strategic Allocation Framework can help you decide where to invest your limited resources in just six steps.

1. **Resource inventory:** You can't allocate what you don't track. Start to understand what you actually have.
2. **Goal clarity:** What are you trying to accomplish? Keep in mind, this is not a list of what you *should* be trying to accomplish. What matters to you right now?
3. **Activity audit:** List everything you do regularly, such as meetings, projects, committees, networking, mentoring, household management, caregiving—everything. For each activity, ask yourself four questions:

- Does it advance one of my top three goals?
- What's the ROI?
- What's the energy cost?
- Can someone else do this?

4. **Strategic cuts:** Identify activities to cut completely, such as
   - Activities that have no connection to your goals + low ROI + high energy costs
   - Activities that are not required + negative ROI
   - Activities that others could do better + you're doing out of habit
5. **Strategic delegation:** What could others do that you are doing? Delegation isn't just for work. It's for life. Strategic delegation is how to protect resources for what matters most.
6. **Strategic investment:** Now that you have reclaimed your time, energy, and attention, where do you invest your newly freed resources?
   - High-ROI professional activities, based on the research offered earlier in this chapter. Focus your attention on activities that allow for the following:
     - Building relationships with decision-makers
     - High-visibility projects aligned with your goals
     - Strategic committee work with real influence
     - Deep work in your area of expertise
     - Conversations with sponsors and advocates

- High-ROI personal activities. Note that these are not luxuries but investments in sustainable performance:
  - Sleep seven to eight hours.
  - Eat nutritious meals sitting down.
  - Exercise regularly.
  - Obtain mental health support, such as from community programs or therapy.
  - Share meaningful time with people you love.
  - Partake in activities that restore your well-being.

Boundary Setting as Revolutionary Leadership

Sometimes, boundaries are misunderstood. Boundaries are not about limitation for the sake of limitation. Rather, they are about exercising leadership. When you set boundaries, you make strategic choices about where you deploy your resources for maximum impact.

Setting boundaries as a Revolutionary Pathmaker involves reframing *no* as power. When you say no to the wrong things, you create the capacity to say yes to the right things. When you protect your energy, you can show up powerfully when it matters most.

Boundary Setting as a Core Leadership Competency

If you are new to healthy boundary setting, I can almost guarantee that it feels hard for you as a Black woman. Do you know why that is? Black women have been socialized to believe that saying no is selfish. We've been taught that we should be able to handle everything and that our strength is infinite. And we've been taught that needing support is a weakness and boundaries disappoint people.

The truth is, this discomfort, or even fear, about setting healthy boundaries is not unfounded. Black women face real consequences when we set boundaries. We are labeled "not a team player," miss out on opportunities, are seen as difficult, face backlash for not carrying invisible labor, and feel guilt for prioritizing ourselves.

However, the research shows that women who set boundaries advance faster than women who don't. This is because they have the energy to perform well when it matters. They focus on high-impact activities, and they model sustainable leadership.[121]

Boundary-Setting Progression

With some resolve and a little courage, you can begin to reclaim your resources and set effective boundaries. However, you don't go from where you are to saying no to everything overnight. We must start small and build our boundary-setting capacity from there. Here's a starting point:

Level 1: Note the obvious—things that clearly don't serve your goals.

Level 2: Say no to the good but not great—opportunities that are good but not aligned with your current goals. This is harder.

Level 3: Say no to the should—things you should do, but you can't do them all. Choosing where you engage is strategic, not selfish. This is the hardest level.

121 Brown, "Revolutionary Evidence."

If, like many of us, your sense of compassion gives you pause, consider the following approach to saying no without burning bridges:

- **Use the direct no:** For example, you can say, "I can't take this on right now," or "I have other commitments." No explanation is needed, and no justification is required.
- **Employ the strategic redirect:** For example, say, "This isn't aligned with my current priorities, but have you considered [another person/approach]?"
- **Use the conditional yes:** For example, say, "I can't do X, but I could do Y." Y is a smaller commitment that you feel is acceptable for you.
- **Consider a time-bound no:** For example, say, "Not right now, but revisit with me in X days' time, when my plate is clear." This is a values-based no, where you've made a commitment to focus on other priorities, and this opportunity or offer doesn't fit that focus.

Featured Resources

If you require further aids in becoming more effective in your engagement efforts, check out the Strategic Engagement strategy featured on https://revolutionarylead.com/.

KEY TAKEAWAYS

- You don't have to do everything to be exceptional. You just must do the right things exceptionally well.

- Working twice as hard isn't the strategy. Working strategically is.
- Saying no to the wrong things creates capacity to say yes to the right things.
- Protecting your resources isn't selfish; it's revolutionary leadership.
- Your health, energy, and peace matter—not just for you, but for everyone who needs you to lead sustainably.
- Revolutionary resource management isn't about doing less. It's about doing what matters more.

ACTION STEPS

- Complete one week's time-and-energy tracking. Identify one activity to cut immediately.
- Track your health matrix—i.e., sleep, meals, exercise. Redefine your boundaries based on what's not working.

PART 3

Transforming Cultures

CHAPTER 10

From Subject to Visionary Architect

Every great dream begins with a dreamer. Always remember, you have within you the strength, the patience, and the passion to reach for the stars to change the world.

HARRIET TUBMAN

In part 2, we discussed strategic power and how you can step into yours. Here, in part 3, we will discuss how you can transform culture. We begin this discussion by learning how you can transform from subject to visionary architect in the systems you find yourself operating in.

Before we go further, it is important we understand what we mean by the terms *subject* and *architect* in this context. A subject is someone systems happen to, an individual who must adapt, navigate, and survive. This person's success depends on learning enough of the rules to advance despite them. An architect is someone who designs systems, transforms them, and creates or builds other systems.

CASE STUDY: REAL DEI

If Black women were free, it would mean that everyone else would have to be free since our freedom would necessitate the destruction of all the systems of oppression.

BARBARA SMITH

At some point in my career, I was hired to "do diversity." It was my job to fix the pipeline, get more Black women in, and help them succeed. In the first six months, I designed programs, ran workshops, created resource groups, and tracked matrices. We started seeing the numbers improve ... but just slightly.

Leadership was pleased. I was exhausted.

You see, I knew the truth: We were treating symptoms, not causes. The problem wasn't that Black women needed training. The problem was the culture. It wasn't designed for these women to thrive. But my role was designed to fix the people, not the system.

Instead, I chose transformation.

I started asking different questions. Not, "How do we help Black women succeed here?" but rather, "What about this culture makes it hard?" The pushback was immediate. I was told that it was not my role, to just stay in my lane. I heard that regularly. Fortunately, I had built enough credibility to push back strategically. I collected data such as cultural patterns, exit interviews, and promotion disparities. My goal was not to share, but to illuminate. I built coalitions and found unexpected allies in people ready for real change. I created proof points. Piloted new approaches. Showed what was possible when systems changed. Within a year and a half, my role had transformed. I was running diversity initiatives. I was redesigning performance systems, restructuring hiring, and shifting decision-making norms.

This was not because someone gave me authority. It was because I had built influence, used it, and become an architect instead of a program manager. The shift from subject to architect didn't require permission; it required strategic action.

POWER ACTIVATION PROMPT

What if you stopped asking "How do I succeed in this system?" and started asking "How do I change this system?" This is the difference between being subject to systems and being the architect of systems.

The Subject-to-Architect Shift

Based on the given definitions of subject and architect and the case study that illustrated the concept, if you are a subject in a system, your goal ought to be to shift toward being an architect. If you decide to make the shift, your impact is measured by how well the system changes, not how much you adapt to it. If we take a closer look at the definitions again, you may note that Black women start out as subjects. This is because we must—the systems we enter aren't designed for us. Our survival requires navigation. But survival isn't the end goal; transformation is. Therefore, the shift from subject to architect happens when we move from trying to succeed in the system to trying to change it.

Defining the Transition

To make the shift, you must first define the transition. There is a difference between learning to navigate a broken system and fixing the system, between adapting to a toxic culture and transforming the culture. Proving that you belong and changing who belongs and gets promoted within the structure are, in turn, different as well. Once you define the transition, you *must* get permission. But you don't obtain permission from anyone other than yourself because nobody else will give it to you.

It is vital to realize that not every system is worth transforming. Not every battle is yours to fight. Sometimes the revolutionary act is leaving. Other times, staying is transforming.

It is vital to realize that not every system is worth transforming. Not every battle is yours to fight. Sometimes the revolutionary act is leaving. Other times, staying is transforming.

Historical Context

Black women have always been architects, not just subjects. The proof points are in the following:

- **During enslavement:** Black women created underground networks, not just as survival systems but as resistance systems. They didn't navigate oppression; they built pathways to freedom.
- **During reconstruction:** Black women built schools when education was denied. They created churches when worship was controlled. They established mutual aid societies when

support was withheld. Black women were not subjects waiting for access. They were architects building alternatives.

- **During Jim Crow:** Black women organized economic boycotts, registered voters, and filed lawsuits. They transformed legal and economic systems from positions with no formal power.
- **During the Civil Rights Movement:** Black women strategized campaigns, trained activists, and built coalitions. They didn't just participate; they designed a movement.
- **As corporate pioneers:** Black women created mentoring networks when formal programs excluded them. They built alternative pathways when official ones were blocked. And they transformed cultures from the margins.

The pattern is clear; Black women don't wait for permission to transform systems. We build influence, create proof points, mobilize coalitions, design alternatives, and make the old way obsolete.

The Influence-Building Framework

We don't need authority to transform systems; we need influence. Influence is how we build power from the margins. To grow your influence, you need to accumulate four types of capital:

1. **Credibility capital:** This is your reputation for competence, reliability, and results. Credibility capital is necessary because people listen to those who have proven that they can deliver. You need undeniable expertise to earn the right to challenge systems.
   WAYS TO BUILD IT:
   - Excel at your actual job.

- Create proof points.
- Document your impact.
- Build expertise in strategic areas.
- Be consistent.

2. **Relational capital:** This is the asset you gain when you grow your network of relationships across differences in hierarchy. Transformation is collective. You need allies, sponsors, peers, and coalitions. Change happens through relationships.

   WAYS TO BUILD IT:

   - Build across, not just up.
   - Find unexpected allies.
   - Be a connector.
   - Invest in reciprocity.
   - Build outside your organization.

3. ***Cultural capital:*** This is your understanding of how power works in your system. You can't transform what you don't understand. Cultural capital is knowing the formal rules and the informal dynamics.

   WAYS TO BUILD IT:

   - Learn the language of the system or community.
   - Understand the incentives.
   - Map the informal power.
   - Know the history.

4. **Moral capital:** This is your ability to articulate a vision that transcends individual interests. People follow those who stand for something beyond themselves. Moral capital makes transformation compelling, not just strategic.

   WAYS TO BUILD IT:

   - Stand for something clear.
   - Connect to shared value.
   - Tell compelling stories.
   - Be consistent in your values.
   - Make it bigger than yourself.

Featured Resources

If you would like additional resources that offer a step-by-step approach to becoming a revolutionary architect, find the *Revolutionary Architect's Toolkit* on my website. This toolkit has five strategies that work to build influence and create transformation from a marginalized position:

1. **Trojan horse:** Use accepted frameworks to introduce revolutionary ideas.
2. **Proof point:** Offer undeniable evidence of what's possible.
3. **The coalition:** Build power through collective action and strategic alliances.
4. **The alternative:** This is when you build what should exist alongside what does exist.
5. **The inside–outside game:** Work on multiple pressure points simultaneously.

Cost of Leading Transformation

1. **Professional costs:** Sometimes you may experience slower advancement because you are labeled "difficult" or "political." You may face extra scrutiny of your work and backlash from those invested in the status quo. Energy spent on transformation work on top of your actual job can be taxing.
2. **Personal costs:** You may experience mental and emotional exhaustion as you carry others' hopes and expectations. Being the face of change may cast you as the target of resistance. Some of your relationships may be strained by different values. You will also have less time for personal priorities.
3. **Psychological costs:** You may face doubts about whether it's worth it, isolation when you are ahead of the curve, and frustration at the slow pace of change. It is not uncommon to experience grief over what won't change fast enough and anger at having to do the work at all.

Revolutionary architects measure impact through transformation: individual awareness, behavioral change, and systemic shifts in organizational culture.

Finally, it's crucial you understand that if you are going to make an impact, it ought to be an impact that matters. Most organizations measure and define DEI by the number of programs or initiatives, but truth is, activities are not equal to making an impact. Revolutionary architects measure impact through transformation: individual awareness, behavioral change, and systemic shifts in organizational culture.

KEY TAKEAWAYS

- You don't need permission to be an architect; you need influence. Influence is built strategically.
- Black women have been doing revolutionary assessments for generations. We call it survival.
- We have tracked which managers promoted us, which companies treated us fairly, which strategies worked, and which barriers persisted. We protected this information and used it strategically.
- Now we're making that evidence impossible to ignore. Not because we need to prove we belong but because organizations need to prove they've changed.
- Data is the difference between transformation and performance.
- Measure what matters. Track what's true. Demand accountability for what the evidence reveals. That's how revolutionary change happens.

ACTION STEPS

- Identify one system you want to transform. Articulate why this transformation matters.
- Build your coalition: Have five strategic conversations.
- Map the formal and informal power in your system.
- Assess your sustainability and resilience.

CHAPTER 11
Revolutionary Evidence

The success of every woman should be an inspiration to another. We should raise each other up. Make sure you're courageous, be strong, be extremely kind, and above all, be humble.

SERENA WILLIAMS

Revolutionary evidence is data that reveals the truth instead of supporting comfortable narratives. It is what Black women have been collecting for generations while systems have been measuring the wrong things—or refusing to measure at all.

POWER ACTIVATION PROMPT

Think about the last diversity report you saw at your organization. The one with charts showing hiring numbers and demographic breakdowns. The one that made everything look like progress.

Now answer this: Did that report measure whether Black women actually got promoted, whether they stayed past year three, whose ideas got credit in meetings, and who had sponsors with actual power?

CASE STUDY: THE NUMBERS

We are better than we think and not yet what we want to be.
NIKKI GIOVANNI

In 2010,[122] *I surveyed 348 Black women across industry and job levels for my PhD dissertation research. Of these participants, 60 percent held master's degrees or higher; 19 percent held doctorate degrees. They worked in twenty-seven different industries. They were qualified by every traditional measure. Yet, Black women still make up only 2–3 percent of senior leadership in most sectors.*

The gap isn't preparation. Rather, it's what organizations choose to measure.

The Data Revolution Black Women Built

For us to fully understand the groundwork Black women have done throughout generations, we must understand the data, beginning with the historical context.

122 Jones, "Quantitative Study."

HISTORICAL CONTEXT

Black women have been building revolutionary evidence for generations. They've done so through church networks, where information was shared about which companies had real advancement paths; affinity organizations, which would document compensation gaps and promotion timelines; and as individuals, keeping logs of whose ideas got credit. Black women needed to base important career decisions on documented facts but because this information did not exist, they had to collect it. Organizations and systems measured what made them look good. Black women measured what was actually true.

UNDERGROUND RESEARCH NETWORKS

When we talk of underground research networks, we mean the affinity organizations that popped up in the USA, such as the National Black MBA Association and the Executive Leadership Council. These were not just networking groups; they were research collectives. Members shared data about which companies promoted women to senior roles, the attrition rates for Black women, and the real reasons why Black women departed their roles. They had to collect this information themselves because the companies wanted to erase their data.

WHY WE HAD TO COUNT OURSELVES

Black women had to accumulate data, both informally and formally. Even this book, and the research it is derived from, is an example of this reality. My 2010 dissertation[123] was based on a group-specific application for Black women because there was a gap in the literature. There were no studies that looked at Black women, specifically for Black women. What was out there was always Black women in

123 Jones, "Quantitative Study."

comparison to other groups or Black women as a part of "women" or as a part of "women of color."

The Cost of Invisible Barriers

When it comes to tracking data, traditional systems—across the board, not just in workplaces—really miss what matters because they don't measure the right things. Typically, they count hiring numbers, retention percentages, training completion rates, and satisfaction scores on surveys that people don't trust. They do not track why people leave their system or why some people are not in the system. They do not track work perspectives, who gets assigned to high-visibility projects, and who gets credited in meetings. They do not track who gets developmental feedback versus criticism. They do not care to know who gets sponsored by decision-makers and who gets to network without sacrificing their family time.

Why Pretty Numbers Don't Work

That colorful report, that impressive PowerPoint presentation, and that public-facing data often look impressive. However, beyond appearing impressive, there is no value in the data these offer.

THE DIVERSITY-THEATER PROBLEM

In many instances throughout my career—whether I was consulting, employed, or sitting on company boards—the Black women I knew at these organizations were planning their exits. Even despite these organizations celebrating their DEI achievements. At a glance, the DEI presentations looked and sounded impressive, and the commitment statements were always strong. But when I interviewed the Black women who worked at these places, something became clear to me: a gap. There was a gap between what was espoused and what was lived. The numbers said progress, but experience said otherwise.

CASE STUDY: THE PROMOTION THAT PROVED NOTHING

Black women ain't bitter. They are just tired of being expected to settle for less.
ISSA RAE

In 2021, I took on a new midsize financial services client who had brought me in to assess its advancement pipeline for women of color. At the time, this company had promoted three Black women to the role of vice president. This, naturally, led the company to celebrate its diversity wins.

The truth behind those promotions emerged quickly, though. It turned out that all three women had been promoted after threatening to leave, and not because the company recognized their talent. The fact that these ladies had competing offers, and the company couldn't afford to lose them, especially during this moment of major commitments around equity, forced the company's hand.

None of these women had sponsors advocating for their next promotion. Each had vice president titles but not the high-profile projects that led to senior vice president roles and beyond. Their compensation was 20 percent or more below that of the white men at the same level. The company promoted them without correcting the pay gap. To add insult to injury, they were not invited to strategy meetings where senior leaders made decisions. Their impressive titles did not grant them the access they needed to get ahead.

While I was consulting for this company, two of these Black women were already interviewing elsewhere; they knew this senior leadership role was just window dressing. Six months later, two of the three women had left.

The company recorded its departures as voluntary attrition with no connection to diversity outcomes. At the same time, the third vice president was isolated and being set up to fail.

Yet, in that year's diversity report, the company celebrated promoting three Black women to the position of vice president.

When those women left, leadership was surprised. They had done everything according to their matrix. The reality was that their matrix measured performance, not transformation.

What the Research Actually Shows

Across 2010[124] and 2025,[125] one pattern remains clear: What organizations choose to measure rarely reflects the conditions Black women are expected to navigate. Revolutionary evidence challenges this gap by revealing not only outcomes but the systems that shape them, evidence that names the barriers to access, relational burden, and structural inequality that traditional organizational metrics overlook.

124 Jones, "Quantitative Study."

125 Brown, "Revolutionary Evidence."

In the 2010 research, internal visibility emerged as a meaningful factor in career advancement for Black women. But the real insight was not simply that visibility mattered; it was that access to visibility itself was unevenly distributed. Advancement was linked to proximity to senior leaders, access to high-exposure projects and informal spaces where decisions were shaped, and relationships that legitimized one's contributions. Many Black women delivered high levels of performance while remaining structurally distant from these arenas. Organizational assessment frameworks, focused primarily on output and performance behavior, captured activity—but not access. What appeared as insufficient readiness was, in many cases, insufficient opportunity.

Fifteen years later, the mechanics of work had changed, but the underlying patterns persisted. Remote and hybrid environments shifted visibility into virtual channels and matrixed reporting structures, expanding the emotional and relational labor required to sustain presence and influence. Internal visibility still mattered, but it now demanded intentional relationship maintenance across multiple spheres, with little acknowledgment of the additional effort involved. Meanwhile, organizational narratives had evolved from diversity language to belonging language—yet belonging was still rarely measured as a structural condition. It appeared as a climate sentiment rather than a question of who holds power, who receives sponsorship, and whose work is recognized and resourced.

The imagery had changed and the language modernized to reflect broader representation. But the core mechanisms through which advancement occurred—sponsorship relationships, selective access to stretch opportunities, and concentrated decision-making authority—remained largely intact. The story the organization told about itself had shifted; the structure shaping Black women's experience had not.

Across both eras, the research makes visible a persistent disjuncture between progress narratives and lived realities. Institutions made the easy changes—messaging, training language, visual representation—while leaving intact the systems that govern opportunity distribution. Revolutionary evidence does not ask whether Black women are present in leadership spaces. It asks whether they are supported, resourced, and able to thrive—and whether the structures surrounding them are willing to account for the labor, care, and relational responsibility that their leadership is too often expected to absorb.

Assessment Frameworks That Tell the Truth

What we need are assessment frameworks that do a good job at telling the truth. There must be an understanding about what actually needs to be measured because real transformation requires measuring what matters.

It is not about how many Black women get hired but about how many advance beyond the entry level. Knowing how many Black women are served is not as important as knowing how many Black women are thriving because of an intervention or service.

Use this QR code to access four assessment frameworks that measure the things that matter:

- **The Advancement Velocity Assessment:** Track how quickly people move through an organization or system by demographic.
- **The Access Audit:** Measure actual access, not theoretical opportunities.
- **The Real Retention Analysis:** Collect exit data with context.
- **The Credit Attribution Study:** Measure whose idea gets implemented, who gets credit, and whose contribution is valued.

Managing the Pushback

Building and showcasing revolutionary evidence attracts pushback. Organizations often resist assessment because leadership knows what the data will show, and they would rather not let it be known. Resistance is a tactic to maintain plausible deniability. Thankfully, there are strategies to overcome this resistance.

Analyze organizational pushback: Use the data to build strategies and interventions for moving forward. A real assessment of why organizations resist allows you to understand and productively counter this resistance, helping to create transformation.

Make the cost of ignorance visible: Show leadership what it costs to ignore the problem. Show them the loss of talent, the revenue gap between the organization's current and potential performance, the reputational risk for not addressing known problems before they become public, and the legal exposure. Make the case for truth telling stronger than the case for avoiding the issue.

Start small; build momentum: You don't need to implement everything at once. Begin with one solution that addresses the most visible gap. Use that to create momentum for deeper transformation. When leadership sees one gap clearly, they are more open to looking for others.

Center those most affected: Centering affected voices makes resistance harder to maintain. Centering those most affected means recording experiences, documenting patterns, and presenting findings. This may look like creating confidential forms where people can share their experiences and where feedback is not sanitized or filtered.

Tie assessment to accountability: Link assessment findings to things that matter, such as compensation, promotion decisions, resource allocations, and strategic priorities. Remember: Measurement without consequences is performative.

KEY TAKEAWAYS

- Create your own evidence. Don't wait for a system to measure what matters.
- Build a research collective. Connect with other Black women to collect information, and share it strategically.
- Demand a better matrix. When you see reports that don't measure up to what matters, name it.
- Make evidence impossible to ignore. When you have data showing disparities, present it strategically.
- Evidence forces responses; complaints don't.

ACTION STEPS

- Document your contributions and outcomes, including the dates and details.
- Build relationships with other Black women who are tracking similar patterns.
- Prepare evidence-based advancement conversations with specific data.

CHAPTER 12
Revolutionary Transformation in Motion

Self-definition and self-validation are not luxuries; they form the bedrock of the journey toward empowerment.
PATRICIA HILL COLLINS

This chapter is somewhat different from previous ones. Here, we zero in on a few excellent real-world examples from Black women. We also briefly discuss scenarios you may encounter, including when change fails and why, success strategies you can employ, and a revolutionary blueprint that will give you the edge.

Revolutionary transformation can be defined as the systemic change that redistributes power. This is not just representation. It is measured by who has the authority to make decisions and who has access to advancement opportunities and equitable outcomes. It is not measured by statistics such as diversity training, completion rates, or hiring numbers. Because the truth is, those statistics are just performative change, and performative change produces surface-level initiatives that create the appearance of progress without addressing the structural barriers.

In most cases, transformation doesn't happen the way some annual reports claim, especially when we think about reporting on the success of Black women or people of color. But as we outlined in the previous chapter, Black women have documented the gaps that couldn't be dismissed. They also built alliances that couldn't be ignored and pushed for accountability that couldn't be avoided.

Often, revolutionary transformation happens when a Black woman somewhere decides she is done with the performance and makes the truth impossible to ignore. She collected evidence that other players in the system couldn't dismiss. She built alliances they couldn't ignore. And she pushed for accountability that couldn't be avoided.

Sometimes, this Revolutionary Pathmaker got credit for this work. Oftentimes, she didn't, but the transformation happened because she refused to stop.

POWER ACTIVATION PROMPT

Can you name a Black woman who documented the gaps your company ignored? Do you know which executive tried to block the audits that were looking under the hood?

Has a Black woman told you how long she's worked to build the case for change? Did she mention she left six months after the transformation because it almost broke her?

Are you protecting the Black women who are doing this work now from retaliation, or are you celebrating the results without acknowledging what it cost?

Black Women Who Lead the Revolution

Let us look at three different case studies that illustrate several lessons we must learn.

CASE STUDY: EVIDENCE-BASED REVOLUTION

If you have some power, then your job is to empower somebody else.
TONI MORRISON

Maya, a vibrant professional in the financial services sector, joined a firm in 2017 as its first Black vice president. At the end of three months, she realized that its celebration of diversity was just a performance. There, Black women were 8 percent of the workforce and represented only 2 percent of management. Close to 65 percent left for greener pastures within three years. She also noted that recommendations by her or other Black women would often be dismissed, while the same recommendations would be praised if delivered by a man. When Maya realized all this, she took to building extensive documentation, particularly of her recommendations, and she persevered even with the occasional pushback she faced when she requested support.

Then the George Floyd incident happened in 2020. The death of a Black man at the hands of white law enforcement catapulted the company—and the country—into a new awakening.

Maya was ready. She recommended a thorough strategic plan that included the investment of several million dollars into a budget for compensation equity. The CEO pushed back initially, but the idea of having to explain to the board a lack of investment toward a new priority quickly changed his mind. He approved the funding.

In the first ninety days, the compensation gap closed because of the money Maya had requested, and the company saw an immediate positive impact. Some of Maya's recommendations were unpopular and caused disagreements with some of the vice presidents who had been mandated, courtesy of Maya's input, to sponsor underrepresented groups. This was because their compensation packages were now tied to corporate social responsibility. Executives who refused to follow the recommendations were offered the opportunity to leave instead of being fired.

While many of the recommendations Maya made reaped excellent results, they also made Maya quite unpopular. But the positive results spoke for themselves: The numbers of Black women in management increased from 2 percent to 9 percent, and the retention rate increased from 35 percent to 71 percent.

However, the cost of these efforts, from microaggressions toward her in the workplace to the negative impact of seventy-hour workweeks on her marriage, was devastating. Ultimately, after having achieved undeniable success at this firm, Maya knew it was time she left.

Not only did Maya make her exit, but she started her own firm, which continues to thrive to this day. Now she has her own practice where she helps other Black women lead transformations without sacrificing themselves, similar to the work that I do.

CASE STUDY: ACADEMIC REVOLUTION

Do not desire to fit in. Desire to oblige yourselves to lead.
GWENDOLYN BROOKS

In 2016, Dr. Chen became the first Black woman to be appointed dean at a prestigious business school. Within her first semester, she understood why that was: Nobody had wanted this job.

It was a punishing role. Faculty ignored directives. The board's chairperson went around her budget. Dr. Chen's authority was essentially theoretical. Worse still, her qualifications and credentials for holding this role were being questioned.

Dr. Chen began collecting data and found that, at her university, only 3 percent of the faculty were Black women, none of whom were full professors. Black women had a little over eight and a half years to tenure, versus five years for white men. Salary offers made to Black women were sometimes up to 20 percent lower than those made to their non-Black counterparts. Equally peculiar was the fact that Black female students had lower grades despite similar GMAT scores. This was the experience of Black women lecturers and Black women students. Dr. Chen presented this data to the institution's top leadership, and her findings were rejected. Leadership even accused her of race-baiting and undermining academic freedom.

Somehow, unbeknownst to Dr. Chen, news of this contentious discussion was leaked to the students. These revelations of injustice caused a huge uproar among the students that even caught mass media attention.

Eventually, the provost came to Dr. Chen and accused her of creating this chaos. Fortunately, Dr. Chen had not only documented the problems; she had spent time working on solutions. She diligently worked on and proposed a comprehensive plan. When the faculty rejected it, she went to the board for approval. It was implemented despite the resistance from faculty.

When Dr. Chen's plan was adopted, some senior members of the faculty could not get on board and chose to resign. She replaced them. And of course, some were dismissed. Some sued. Some of those suits were settled.

Despite all this upheaval and disruption, Dr. Chen's plan worked. By 2023, the number of Black women on the faculty had climbed to 11 percent. There were two full professors. The tenure gap was reduced from three and a half years to much less. Further still, these positive outcomes were normalized.

But again, there were costs to Dr. Chen: death threats, daily racist attacks, and isolation from her colleagues. This took such a toll on her that she developed chronic health issues because of the stress. Her marriage suffered, and ultimately, she and her husband divorced. The faculty allies she thought she had stayed silent when things got ugly for her.

When Dr. Chen eventually left the institution, several years later, the improvements remained in place.

CASE STUDY: TECH STARTUP TRANSFORMATION

I do not weep at the world—
I am too busy sharpening my oyster knife.
ZORA NEALE HURSTON

Keisha was another "first": the first Black woman to take on the role of vice president of engineering at a growing tech startup in 2019. In this role, she led a department of two hundred engineers, only 4 percent of whom were Black women and none of whom were in engineering leadership.

This was during the era when diversity was "it," and the company's founders wanted to be inclusive or at least said they did. Fortunately for Keisha, she had an important advantage: The organization was new. So she was able to track demographics from day one, building equity from the ground up before negative patterns could calcify.

Unlike Maya and Dr. Chen—and most Black women in established organizations with embedded inequities and a resistant leadership—Keisha really didn't face any resistance.

When Change Fails and Why

From my observations, when well-laid plans for transformation fail, there are three reasons: You have been set up to fail, your title is just symbolic—you have no real power—or the company has chosen to preserve its reputation rather than expose ugly truths.

Extracting Success Strategies

The following are three strategies that can help you find success in the systems you operate in despite organizational pushback.

WHAT MADE THE DIFFERENCE

Maya used a crisis as leverage. She had built a case before George Floyd's murder and the racial reckoning that followed. So when the CEO wanted to accelerate change, Maya was able to be clear about what she wanted and demand what was required.

The lesson? When pressure creates an opening, we must be ready. We must be specific and make the transformation big enough to matter.

Dr. Chen went to the board when the faculty rejected her proposal because she knew where the real power lives.

The lesson? We must find the people with the power to support change and engage them in it.

Keisha was building equity into systems first, instead of trying to retrofit systems for equity. She started with systems, not training.

The lesson? If you can do so, build equity in from the beginning.

RESISTANCE TACTICS AND HOW TO COUNTER THEM

This transformation work typically faces resistance, such as reverse discrimination claims.

To counter that, we can expand existing practices, including equity, to everyone. Therefore, if there is an existing practice that some people don't have, everyone could get access to it.

PROCESS CONCERN TROLLING

You may experience concern trolling, and to counter it, you must present disparities. That way, you are questioning processes rather than addressing them.

"CHANGE IS TOO EXPENSIVE"

Critics often claim that the company cannot afford equity programs. Yes, interventions can be expensive. However, they are often less resource intensive than recruiting or marketing—in other words, it's less expensive to retain Black women than it is to replace them.

"YOU'RE BEING DIVISIVE"

When those resisting claim that you are being divisive, remind them that division already exists. Point to the data. The division isn't created when you name it. The division exists in the outcomes. Your evidence makes it impossible to ignore. That's what they are uncomfortable with. The lesson? Don't accept blame for revealing problems you didn't create. Show your critics the data that proves division already existed. You just made it measurable.

WHEN TO STAY, WHEN TO LEAVE

Black women often find themselves debating whether it's worth staying and doing this work or if they're better off just leaving. The presence or absence of several factors can show you whether you should stay or leave. Staying is likely the better option when the system or organization has made a real commitment with resources and there are allies willing to take risks. It's the better option when change is visible and not just behind the scenes, when people are telling you that the system is changing, and when you believe you are protected from retaliation.

On the other hand, leaving is the better option when promises don't materialize, when you are feeling isolated, and when truth brings retaliation. When you're holding so much that your health is beginning to suffer, that's a clear sign that this system is no longer good for you. When the culture remains toxic, it is time to leave.

Sometimes we hold leaving as failure, but sometimes it's the most revolutionary choice. Protecting yourself is revolutionary too.

Your Revolutionary Blueprint

When it comes to implementing the *revolutionary blueprint*, you will find yourself in one of two scenarios: You are either leading a transformation or navigating a system as a regular participant.

IF YOU ARE LEADING TRANSFORMATION

If you are leading a system, start with one ninety-day barrier. In the case of Maya, it was compensation equity. For Dr. Chen, it was the evaluation bias. For Keisha, it was the hiring process.

Don't just study what needs to be done; implement it. Build coalitions before you need them. Know who has the power, and build those relationships now. Ask for real resources, such as a budget, genuine accountability, real consequences, and rewards.

Know when the cost becomes too high, set healthy boundaries, and build support. And know your exit timeline and when enough is enough—and when it's time to leave.

IF YOU'RE NAVIGATING A SYSTEM

Assess honestly, and ask yourself these questions: Is a situation real or just a performance? Are there consequences for leadership if things don't come to fruition? Does resource allocation align with the priorities the company espouses? Are Black women protected? Build your engagement based on reality. If it's performative, perhaps just protect your energy and build other options.

Always have an updated evidence portfolio. This is where you track contributions, document your barriers, and connect with other Black women—something we don't do often enough because the systems have pitted us against each other. You can choose to erase that program.

When the cost is too high, you must be aware of it, and you should transition. But if you do refuse to participate in this performativity, you must plan ahead. There is no shame in protecting yourself.

KEY TAKEAWAYS

- Document everything before you need it. Start now; there's no better time.
- Use external pressure strategically: Know what forces your organization to care about things, and build relationships accordingly.
- Make resistance visible and costly: Connect the costs to a cost leadership cares about.
- Force a choice between transformation and resistance.
- Protect yourself from the start. Put your mask on before you help others. That may mean getting a therapist, building an external network, setting boundaries, and knowing your exit plan. You need to get these things before you need them.
- Revolutionary transformation is possible. Maya proved it, Dr. Chen proved it, and Keisha proved it. But it's rare.

- When transformation requires discomfort, most organizations choose performative actions. Women who have succeeded read the context. They made strategic moves. They built alliances, they demanded resources, and they knew their own limits. Women who have failed were set up. They were given titles without power, blamed for the conditions, and held back from succeeding.
- Protecting yourself is as revolutionary as transforming systems. Both matter, both are necessary, and both are your choice. So choose wisely.

ACTION STEPS

- Choose one barrier you've experienced within the ninety days and assess if the transformation is real.
- Identify allies with power, and determine your engagement level in advance.
- Build your evidence portfolio.

CHAPTER 13
Revolutionary Cultural Architecture

Dreams are lovely. But they are just dreams. Fleeting, ephemeral. Pretty. But dreams do not come true just because you dream them. It's hard work that makes things happen. It's hard work that creates change.

SHONDA RHIMES

In this chapter, we discuss *revolutionary cultural architecture*; that is, the framework within which we can carry out impactful endeavors and work. Revolutionary cultural architecture is the intentional design and redesign of organizational systems, structures, and processes. This type of architecture is far superior to conventional design because it allows for the equal distribution of power and enables revolutionary leadership to thrive.

CASE STUDY: NEW BEGINNINGS

Where there is a woman, there is magic.

NTOZAKE SHANGE

Many years ago, the president of a large firm asked me to lead their racial justice work. At the time, I was already working inside one of the largest labor unions in the country. There, I ran the internal consultancy focused on organizational equity through leadership development.

As it happened, my role in the labor union had already attracted a degree of skepticism from the community. Millions of members, many of them Black with decades of history, publicly questioned whether the organization was fighting for their worker rights.

As I spent three months listening to what the members and other stakeholders had to say, I noted the same patterns. While there was talk of solidarity in the organization, it was clear that decision-making centered on the white members' concerns.

Leadership pipelines moved white leaders, particularly men, into the highest-level roles within the organization. And yes, that was where the power was. Subsequently, I went back with a proposal. I informed the president that though he had tapped me to run this program about racism, it would only work if he allowed me to redesign how the organization functioned around racial dynamics and how the organizational systems worked against it.

Fortunately, the president was receptive to my proposal and elevated me to the president's office to do this work. This change gave me access to actual decision-making. We didn't just create a racial justice program. Rather, we built a center that coordinated with hundreds of local unions to redesign everything from contract negotiations to leadership development. In addition, we changed how locals evaluated candidates, allocated resources, and set bargaining priorities.

Approximately three years in, we started to see positive results. Higher participation from Black members led to an increased number of contracts, which contributed to a growing reflection of Black workers' priorities as the central demand. This result was not because we convinced white members to care more but because we redesigned the systems that determine whose concerns counted.

This approach made all the difference between program and architecture.

POWER ACTIVATION PROMPT

What if the problem isn't the people but the structures they're operating in?

The Architects Who Came Before

Black women don't just survive broken systems; we build new ones. In churches, we created leadership structures when white churches didn't or when they excluded us. We designed something different, something that valued our community along with organizational efficiency.

In schools, we built institutions when public education failed us. And those systems were created from learning that honored our intelligence while addressing our specific needs and our children's needs.

In communities, we designed mutual aid networks when government systems left us behind. There was no charity, just the architecture of systems focused on resource sharing, decision-making, and collective power.

Black women have always been culture architects. We just didn't have the title.

CASE STUDY: SURYA BONALY'S ILLEGAL ACT

It was when I realized I needed to stop trying to be somebody else and be myself, I actually started to own, accept, and love what I had.
TRACEE ELLIS ROSS

It was the Olympics in Japan in 1998, and it was Surya's last chance to participate. Certain sports, such as skating in the Winter Olympics, are notoriously underrepresented when it comes to diversity, particularly back then. So, Surya Bonaly, a Black French ice-skater, was indeed an anomaly.[126] *No stranger to standing out, as a Black woman who had navigated racism in both America and France, she was familiar with overcoming adversity. But this Olympic competition was harder: Not only was it her last opportunity to compete in the Olympics,*[127] *but she was also attempting to perform under extreme pressure, at an international level, while nursing an injury she had not fully recovered from.*

Since 1990, Surya had been winning medals, but there in Japan, in her last championship, the odds were stacked against

126 Mark Kram, "Bonaly, Surya 1973–," *Encyclopedia.com*, accessed January 18, 2026, https://www.encyclopedia.com/education/news-wires-white-papers-and-books/bonaly-surya-1973.

127 Keli Goff, "Figure Skater Surya Bonaly Flipped Her Way into Our Hearts," *The Root*, February 18, 2014, https://www.theroot.com/figure-skater-surya-bonaly-flipped-her-way-into-our-hea-1790874627.

her. The day before her performance at the Winter Olympics, she pulled a muscle that led to her being unable to walk upstairs unassisted. At the same time, she was still recovering from an older injury—a severe rupture of her Achilles.[128]

In a moment that placed her firmly in history as the first person to ever land on one foot from a backflip, in this competition, Surya became a legend. Propelling herself backward with her injured right foot, she landed magnificently on her left.[129] *The only other person who successfully performed a similar move, back in 1976, had landed on both feet. However, soon after, the championship authorities branded Surya's move illegal.*

Even though she lost in this competition, this "landing on one leg" backflip is now referred to by Surya's last name.[130] *Forty-eight years after her championship performance, in 2024, this move became legal.*[131]

Surya did something "illegal" that later became legal. That's the definition of revolutionary cultural architecture. She didn't wait for the system to change. She showed what was possible, and the culture eventually caught up.

---

128 Ibid.

129 Ibid.

130 Ibid.

131 Nick Zaccardi, "From Surya Bonaly to Ilia Malinin, Figure Skating's Backflip Comeback Sparks Reaction," *NBC Sports*, October 16, 2024, https://www.nbcsports.com/olympics/news/figure-skating-backflip-ilia-malinin-surya-bonaly-adam-siao-him-fa.

Three Principles from Black Women's Cultural Building

Design for the margins: Black women never designed for the average user. We designed for people with constraints—people without resources, people navigating hostile systems. When you design for the margins, you build systems that work for everyone.

Build collective power: White male culture celebrates lone geniuses. Black women built differently by designing systems where power was shared, leadership was rotated, and everyone's contribution mattered. We recognized that individual and exclusionary systems are always precarious: You eliminate one person, and you are back to the status quo. But if you spread influence, it becomes collective power.

Create accountability without hierarchy: Traditional organizations assume you need hierarchy to have accountability. Black women built systems with accountability but without rigid hierarchy. In those instances, leadership was distributed, while standards remained high.

The Design Principles of Revolutionary Culture

Cultural architecture is about the foundational systems, structures, and processes that shape how an organization really functions; it's not about the policies on paper. It is about the actual mechanisms that determine who has power, how decisions are made, and who's successful—or whose success that system enables.

According to my research of organizations that work well for Black women, there are four foundations or principles for the design of revolutionary cultural architecture:[132]

- **Transparent systems:** Decision-making criteria, elevation or promotion standards, and resource allocation rationales must be made visible and documented, not hidden or subjective. Research shows that Black women advance faster in organizations with transparent promotion processes. This is not because the bias disappears but because it becomes visible and is subsequently addressed. When promotion decisions are made behind closed doors, biases flourish.
- **Multiple pathways:** Most traditional organizations have one path to success, one that worked for whomever designed it. However, revolutionary cultures can be designed through multiple pathways that lead to the same destination, allowing different ways to demonstrate competence, different timelines for advancement, and different styles of leadership that all count as leadership. My research indicates that Black women thrive in organizations that value internal visibility over external expertise and in organizations that recognize community leadership as equivalent to corporate networking—but only when those things are structurally valued, not just acknowledged.[133]
- **Distributed power:** This is power that is located across multiple points and people in an organization, not concentrated at the top. In a system where there is distributed power, different people have real decision-making authority in their

132 Brown, "Revolutionary Evidence."

133 Ibid.

respective domains. We know that power concentrated at the top means change depends on whoever happens to be sitting in that position. This is the exact opposite of revolutionary cultural architecture, where power is distributed across multiple points.

- **Learning systems:** Design organizations to continuously gather feedback to measure outcomes, and adjust or pivot based on evidence rather than assuming that the initial design was correct. Traditional cultures assume they know what works. Revolutionary cultures assume they are always learning. They build feedback loops, measure what matters, and adjust based on the evidence.

  There is a critical distinction between structural versus programmatic change. Programmatic change adds initiatives, training, or programs to the existing system. Revolutionary cultures pursue structural change. You must change the system itself: the decision-making process, the evaluation criteria, and the research allocations.

Assessing Before Redesigning

You cannot obtain great results if you are not prepared. It is vital that you carry out an assessment before you redesign a cultural architecture. I recommend this three-part assessment:

Part 1: Map decision points. Every organization has points where decisions are made. Most organizations can't tell you who makes decisions at those points. They know who should, but the reality is often different. Map the real, not the official.

Part 2: Track resource flow. Power follows resources: money, time, attention, credibility. Who gets budgets, who gets direct reports, who gets face time, who gets credit for success. Organizations that work for Black women distribute resources based on explicit criteria and not implicit relationships.

Part 3: Identify invisible systems. There are two operating systems in every organization. There is the official one in the handbook, and the real one people follow. The real system includes unwritten rules about how to get ahead, informal networks deciding who gets information, and the cultural norms that dictate whose leadership style counts. Making invisible systems visible is key. The assessment reveals what needs to be redesigned. When you arrive at this point, you are ready for systemic transformation.

The RAISE Framework for Cultural Redesign

When you have carried out the previous assessment, you can now implement the RAISE Framework for Cultural Redesign. The RAISE Framework, my proprietary road map, provides a systematic redesign approach that encompasses five interconnected aspects:

Rooted in authentic leadership: Revolutionary cultures start with real values, not performative ones.

> The architectural move → Design systems that reward authentic leadership, not just leadership that looks familiar. Design in such a way that multiple leadership styles count, different communication approaches are valued, and there are various paths to influence or recognition. My 2025

research[134] shows that organizations where Black women advanced and where they were promoted had elevation criteria that explicitly valued diverse leadership approaches. These were not exceptions but equal standards.

Amplify strategic influence: Revolutionary cultures distribute influence across multiple points, not just to those with titles.

The architectural move → Redesign decision-making structures to include voices from the margins. These are not just communities that advise, or listening sessions, but teams that decide.

Most organizations stop at listening, but revolutionary cultures embrace power sharing.

Inspire collective impact: Revolutionary cultures recognize that sustainable change comes from collective action, not heroic individuals.

The architectural move → Design systems that create collective wins, not just individual advancement. The promotion criteria for these redesigned systems must include the lifting of others, new evaluation systems, rewarding teams alongside individual achievement, and resource allocation that builds collective capacity.

Sustain through equity and care: Revolutionary cultures build sustainability into the design from the start.

The architectural move → Create structures that persist beyond personalities and pressure: distributive leadership that survives transition, feedback loops that are continu-

---

134 Brown, "Revolutionary Evidence."

ous, and accountability systems that operate independently of champions. Organizations that sustain transformation have built equity into operations, into budgets, and into evaluations.

Evaluate and celebrate progress: Revolutionary cultures measure what matters, evaluate progress and celebrate, and adjust based on evidence.

The architecture move → Design measurement systems that track power distribution, not just representation. Measure who makes the decisions, not just who attends meetings. Track who gets resources, not just who gets invited. Recognize whose ideals get implemented, not just whose voices get heard.

Building for the Long Run

Most organizational change fails within two years. But revolutionary culture builds sustainability into the architecture.

Design for leadership transition: Power concentrated at the top means change depends on whoever happens to be sitting in that position. Revolutionary cultures distribute power across multiple points.

Build feedback loops: Revolutionary design builds constant assessment into its operations. When there are unforeseen deviations from a system that previously worked well, it is not because you got it wrong; it's because circumstances change, and the architecture must evolve.

Create reinforcing structures: Culture changes when multiple structures reinforce each other. Therefore, there may be a need to change several functions, such as hiring, promotion, evaluation, and compensation, at the same time. Design systems where doing the right thing is easier than doing the wrong thing.

Planning for resistance: Revolutionary design anticipates resistance. You may experience resistance from three fronts:

1. **People who have benefited from old systems:** Don't try to convince them; design around their resistance and build coalitions with others.
2. **People who are afraid of change:** Address this with transparency. Show how new systems present opportunity and how early adopters model success.
3. **The systems themselves:** Revolutionary design works with organizational logic.

Frame change as consistent with the mission, and make the case in organizational language.

KEY TAKEAWAYS

- Programs change people, but architecture changes systems.
- Black women have always been cultural architects.
- Assessment must come before redesign.
- The RAISE Framework provides systemic transformation. Random changes create random results.
- Sustainability is designed, not hoped for. Most transformation dies within two years because it wasn't built to last.

- Cultural architecture where Black women thrive has four essential foundations: transparent systems, multiple pathways to success, distributed power across levels and learning systems.

ACTION STEPS

- Conduct an architectural audit and map the current organizational architecture and identify redesign opportunities.
- RAISE redesign blueprint: Create a new cultural architecture using the five RAISE components.

CHAPTER 14

Revolutionary Measurement

Invention, discovery, and empires are built of chances taken with high degrees of failure.

STACEY ABRAMS

It's said that if you can't measure it, you can't manage it, and when it comes to being a Revolutionary Pathmaker, this is true. Gathering data, through measurements, is key. When we refer to measurement in this context, we mean tracking what drives your advancement and community progress. Often, this is not what organizations want to celebrate. That is because it measures strategic position or impact instead of activity or effort. It is about measuring what matters, not measuring to impress.

POWER ACTIVATION PROMPT

What if the numbers you're chasing don't matter?

CASE STUDY: WHEN MAYA WAS VISIBLY INVISIBLE

You can be the lead in your own life.
KERRY WASHINGTON

Maya was doing everything right. She was a healthcare professional that contributed her all at work, but she was not getting promoted. It was even more frustrating when she received verbal praise yet had nothing tangible to show for it. Eventually, enough was enough, and she started to do things differently. Chief among the changes she made was a shift to doing more internal visibility tasks. In under six months, she was promoted—twice!

Prior to either promotion, Maya was very busy outside the office. She was taking up speaking engagements, including bookings at four industry conferences. She was writing and publishing articles and had, at that point, published three articles in a trade publication. Her steady effort contributed to her building a following. The company she worked at even featured her several times in their marketing materials.

However, when vice president promotions were announced, Maya was not on the list. Not only had she been a director for four years, but she had watched three of her colleagues with less experience get promoted around her. Maya didn't understand what she was missing.

Maya's colleagues who received promotions had all done exactly what she was doing. Like her, they built visibility, established their expertise, and made the company look good. However, the factor Maya was missing was that she was doing it externally, while her colleagues were doing it internally. Eventually, Maya talked to a mentor of hers, and they told her that nobody at the C-suite level knew who she was. Naturally, Maya was shocked because, as she put it, she "was everywhere." What she had failed to realize was that her presence on panels and her articles in prestigious publications made her visible to the industry but not to the people who could promote her.

When Maya asked me to assist her, one of the first solutions I immediately implemented was an audit of her calendar. We needed to know where all her visibility-related efforts and impact were going. After analyzing the previous six months, we tracked that she had spent forty hours on conference preparation, thirty hours on speaking engagements, and twenty-five hours on writing articles. However, when it came to what mattered—internal meetings with executives—she had only spent four hours. Only four hours, in a span of six months! In total, she was spending ninety-five hours building an external brand and four hours building her reputation with the people who controlled her advancement.

What we discovered through tracking her calendar changed everything. Thankfully, Maya understood that her external brand would not get her promoted but her internal positioning could. She also understood that though the speaking engagements at conferences made her feel good and successful, the strategic projects in the company made her feel equally so. Subsequently, she started declining these requests for external visibility. Then, she accepted a role in a high-visibility task force that the executive team would see on a weekly basis.

As Maya started performing in this high-visibility task force, the CFO started asking for her opinion in meetings. People started to learn from her in strategy sessions. They watched her solve problems that they cared about.

And she finally got promoted ... twice.

By now, we know that Black women don't get promoted based solely on our reputation. Decision-makers promote you on your capability, and they can only promote capability when they see it. You will not be promoted because somebody else told them about you.

Historical Foundations

Historically, Black women measured success differently because they had to. They did not use markers such as titles or money. Black women measured community impact. They tracked how many people they lifted from unfortunate circumstances. They kept score of who got better because they were there. Black women measured collective advancement by tracking how their success created pathways for others.

Alongside collective advancement, Black women also measured cultural preservation. This factor required them to know if they were protecting what mattered while navigating hostile systems. They also measured strategic invisibility, a factor that, as many Black women realized, was a matrix where they were overlooked. And often, being overlooked impacted their safety and survival. They also measured the number of doors opened—the opportunities that had been made available to those who were coming up behind them.

Women who took maternal roles in Black churches often did not hold formal leadership titles. Yet they ran entire congregations. Black teachers typically measure success by the students who made it out. Civil rights organizers counted changed systems, and did not aim for personal recognition.

When you think about this historical context, the efforts of these trailblazers were more than noble sacrifice. They were strategic, because individual advancement without community advancement means nothing. As such, their matrix reflected the mission.

The 60/10 Problem

There is a divide between what organizations measure and what works. This is best encapsulated by the *60/10 problem*. According to the 60/10 problem, most professionals spend 60 percent of their time on activities that contribute only 10 percent to their advancement goals. This happens because organizations measure what they want to celebrate and not what drives advancement.

Some aspects that organizations measure include

- Diversity numbers as they relate to representation
- Employee resource group participation
- External speaking engagements
- Publications
- Professional development courses
- Networking events attendance
- Visible committee work

My research shows what truly predicted advancement were[135]

- internal visibility activities (specifically, accepting highly visible work assignments),
- serving on internal task forces,
- lunch or dinner with supervisors and top executives, and
- physically stopping by the office, with hours worked correlating with promotion.

The paradox is that expert activities approach a negative correlation with advancement: The more time spent building an external brand, the fewer the promotions. Organizations celebrate external visibility but promote internal visibility. External visibility feels revolutionary, and it looks like power, but internal visibility creates power.

Framework: The Revolutionary Matrix

The intent of the *Revolutionary Matrix* is to stop tracking vanity matrices and start measuring strategic position. To successfully measure this matrix, you need the data from five measurement categories:

- **Decision-maker access:** How many decision-makers know your name? How many have seen your work directly? How often are you in rooms where decisions happen?
- **Strategic visibility indicators:** Strategic visibility impact—are you on high-impact projects that leadership cares about? Do decision-makers see you solving problems that matter to them? Are you visible on priorities that affect the bottom line?

135 Jones, "Quantitative Study."; Brown, "Revolutionary Evidence."

- **Internal influence indicators:** Who has asked for your input for important decisions? Who invites you to strategy conversations? Who mentions your name when you are not in the room?
- **Collective progress markers:** How many people advance because of your advocacy? What systems have changed because of your influence? Who has gotten opportunities they wouldn't have had without you?
- **Energy ROI:** Which activities move your position? What are you doing that looks good but changes nothing? Where is the gap between effort and outcome?

RESEARCH INSIGHTS

Across my 2010 research[136] and 2025 research,[137] the clearest finding is not simply which activities correlate with advancement but what Black women must carry for that advancement to occur. Traditional metrics focus on visible outputs—role attainment, promotional movement, external recognition—but they do not account for the access conditions, relational strain, and emotional costs required to sustain those outcomes.

The 2010 research illuminates the foundations of what later became the 60/10 problem. Many Black women were devoting extraordinary time and energy to activities that appeared meaningful—professional development sessions, external speaking engagements, industry recognition—yet past advancement trajectories were most strongly tied to visibility inside the organization. High-exposure assignments, proximity to decision-makers, strategic committee lead-

136 Jones, "Quantitative Study."

137 Brown, "Revolutionary Evidence."

ership, and informal relational presence shaped mobility more than any external accomplishment could. Advancement was less about effort and more about selective access.

The 2025 analysis complicates this pattern. Internal visibility remains structurally influential in promotion decisions—but the research also shows that sustaining internal visibility requires more emotional and relational labor than organizational metrics acknowledge. In remote and matrixed contexts, being visible means continually translating one's contributions across multiple reporting lines, moderating perception, and absorbing representational pressure. What appears in performance systems as leadership readiness often reflects unmeasured stabilization labor—labor disproportionately performed by Black women.

At the same time, activities categorized as low impact in traditional advancement models—such as external speaking, community leadership, or professional reputation building—served a different and equally important function in the 2025 data. These activities supported grounding, identity coherence, creativity, confidence, and peer solidarity. They strengthened the very sense of self and purpose that allowed Black women to remain in leadership at all. External visibility did not fail to produce promotions; rather, promotions were simply not the only—or always the most meaningful—outcome to measure.

Taken together, the research shows that organizations continue to reward behaviors that increase institutional value while under-measuring the relational and emotional costs associated with those behaviors. *Revolutionary measurement* challenges that imbalance. It shifts attention from effort to access, from presence to power, and from organizational output to leadership sustainability. It asks not only, "Which activities accelerate advancement?" but also, "At what costs, under what conditions, and for whose benefit?"

Revolutionary measurement is not about finding the fastest path upward—it is about documenting the truth of what upward movement requires and naming the difference between activities that look powerful and those that actually change position, safety, and possibility.

WHY DOES THIS MATRIX MATTER MORE THAN TRADITIONAL SUCCESS MARKERS?

Traditional markers *feel* productive; the Revolutionary Matrix creates results. Let's consider the average relationship you may have with your senior vice president or other high-level decision-maker. Traditional markers fail because the leaders that you report to don't see your LinkedIn profile. They don't know you have spoken at three conferences. They don't track how many hours you spend at the employee resource group. However, they will remember you when you lead a project at work. They will notice you when you solve that problem. If the CEO sees you in a strategy meeting, they are more likely to promote you.

Stop measuring effort, and start measuring access.

KEY TAKEAWAYS

- Black women have always measured community, while corporations measured competition. We tracked collective progress, while they tracked individual performance. Measure what matters.

- Internal visibility predicts advancement; external visibility doesn't. Decision-makers promote whom they see, not whom they hear about.
- Strategic position matters more than impressive activity.
- Revolutionary measurement includes the collective matrix.
- Energy ROI, the gap between effort and outcome, shows where you are wasting power.

ACTION STEPS

- List your current success matrix, and cross out anything that doesn't give decision-maker visibility.
- Identify three decision-makers who should know your work, and create visibility with one.
- Accept one high-internal-visibility project. Decline one thing that looks impressive but changes nothing.
- Measure collective impact: Who has advanced because of you, and what systems have changed?

PART 4

Legacy and Liberation

CHAPTER 15

Revolutionary Wisdom Activation and Sustainability

You must never be fearful about what you are doing when it is right.

ROSA PARKS

Every Revolutionary Pathmaker has their own type of wisdom that only needs the right triggers to activate and the right environment to last.

CASE STUDY: LETTERS TO MY DAUGHTERS

My mother did not raise me to ask for permission to lead.

AYANNA PRESSLEY

As stated in earlier chapters, I have four children, two of them daughters. As it happens, my girls have a twenty-four-year age gap. One activity I have made a habit of doing for each of them is writing letters to them. This effort was born from an impulse for them to have an easier go of life. I wanted them to have the blueprint where I had none. Often, the questions I asked myself as I prepared to put pen to paper were, "What do I need them to know that I can't teach them in person? What wisdom might they need when I'm not there to offer it?"

Those letters became more than personal guidance. They became a template for how I think about wisdom transmission now. My older daughter, a classically trained ballerina, was navigating a world where she stands out as the anomaly. When she was starting out, there just weren't a lot of Black ballerinas to look up to in the sea of white ballet dancers. I had to offer her the wisdom to build her confidence and power with limited models. I had to advise her on the cost of blazing trails.

For my younger daughter, I write different letters for her unique circumstances. Her letters are about leveraging the past that others, such as her older sister, have created. As a performer herself, she needs to understand the importance of collective power instead of individual exceptionalism. She would benefit from grasping the value of building movements and memories, and not just going through the motions.

Both sets of letters share the same: the truth. Through this, I hope my daughters don't have to repeat my hardest lessons.

And that is how I would define revolutionary wisdom activation and sustainability. Through it, we are documenting what we learned, and we start from where we end it. That's the work of revolutionary wisdom transmission.

Each generation should build—but not from scratch. We must stand on the foundation that has been built. We reach higher heights because we lift each other.

POWER ACTIVATION PROMPT

What knowledge are you carrying that the next generation desperately needs? What would you want them to know that you had to learn the hard way?

The Tradition of "Passing It On"

Black people have been knowledge keepers since time immemorial. From kitchens and church basements and through hushed conversations and careful mentoring. Through these, we modeled for more than what we said.

If we think about our grandmothers, they passed down survival strategies wrapped in stories. Our aunties shared navigation tactics disguised as advice. Our mentors gave us real rules. These were rules that were never written in employee handbooks or company policies. All this transmission happened informally, organically, person to person, and usually outside of official channels.

And it worked—until it didn't, because informal network transfer does have its flaws. It is fragile and depends on proximity. It depends on the relationships that form naturally. Often, it's about being in the right place, at the right time, with the right person. In an organizational context, that means when a Black woman executive leaves, her strategic intelligence leaves too. The women lower down in the organizational hierarchy, who desperately need that knowledge, never get access to it.

As a result, the Black women rising in the ranks are forced to create that strategic intelligence again. We need to do more to ensure this knowledge is transmitted.

Research Validation

Across both research time frames,[138] [139] wisdom was not found in formal leadership pipelines or institutional knowledge systems but in relationships, shared experience, and collective problem-solving. Black women were not lacking access to wisdom; they were generating it constantly in motion, in conversation, in quiet acts of survival and innovation that rarely became part of organizational memory.

The research reveals that the knowledge most essential to navigating leadership—how to sustain visibility without exhaustion, how to build distributed support, how to protect one's humanity inside systems not built to hold it—was not formally transmitted but exchanged laterally and intergenerationally.[140] Much of this wisdom remained lived rather than documented, embodied rather than archived. When women transitioned out of their roles, their strategies often left with them, even as the systems that benefited from their insight remained unchanged.

Revolutionary wisdom, then, is not simple expertise—it is knowledge that is cultivated through care, relationships, and endurance, and it becomes sustainable only when it is shared, protected, and rooted in community rather than extracted by institutions.

138 Jones, "Quantitative Study."

139 Brown, "Revolutionary Evidence."

140 Ibid.

Why Traditional Succession Planning Fails Us

This unplanned approach leads to a failure of succession planning. Traditional succession planning assumes knowledge transfer happens through formal mentoring programs and leadership development initiatives. Yet that planning doesn't account for informal intelligence. Black women handled the mantle to lead the need to know how to read political dynamics, when to push and when to wait, and which battles matter and which ones drain your resources.

Traditional planning also assumes that your successor looks like you and has similar access. This is wrong on both counts for Black women leaders. It assumes you have permission to pass the knowledge down so that your expertise will be valued and preserved. However, Black women often don't get that permission. Our knowledge gets dismissed as soft skills or cultural competence instead of strategic intelligence. Therefore, we need our own transmission systems.

The Knowledge Capture Framework

What wisdom needs documenting? Not everything needs to be written down. Some knowledge stays alive through practice and presence. But certain strategic intelligence must be captured explicitly.

There are four categories in which strategic intelligence or wisdom must be captured.

NAVIGATION INTELLIGENCE

- Which organization systems actually drive advancement
- How to read power dynamics in your specific context
- Which visibility activities increase versus drain energy

- Which activities advance you or put a target on your back

RELATIONSHIP CAPITAL

- Who holds real power versus titles
- How alliances can be built across differences
- Which networks open doors
- How community connections can be leveraged professionally

CULTURAL TRANSLATION

How to make your value visible in dominant culture terms.

- When to code-switch, and when to stay planted
- How to protect your energy while driving change
- How to build power without burning out

CHANGE AGENCY STRATEGY

Which transformation approaches work in resistance transformation systems.

- How to gather evidence that forces conversations
- When to move fast, and when to move slowly
- How to sustain change beyond your tenure

THE LEGACY DOCUMENTATION SYSTEM

These four categories require the capture of significant volumes of data. How is this achieved? Here are some options on how to capture this knowledge systematically to create a legacy documentation system:

- **Create your strategic intelligence archive:** Document the lessons that cost you the most to learn. This should not be general advice; it should be specific, tactical intelligence. What meetings actually mattered? Which relationships opened the most doors? Which battles were worth fighting? Write it down in detail because your future self and successors need specificity.
- **Build your strategic/decision framework library:** You make hundreds of strategic decisions based on pattern recognition that new leaders don't have yet. Capture your decision-making process. When someone asks about your thought process when carrying out a specific task, consider the signals you read, the patterns you recognized, and the framework that guided your choices. Documenting these can turn tacit knowledge into explicit frameworks that others can apply.
- **Map your relationship ecosystem:** My research shows that relationship capital drives advancement.[141] However, people can't see your full network or understand how you built it. Document your key relationships, but go beyond just names. Document how each connection developed, what value you brought to them, how they helped you, and what new leaders need to know about building similar capital. It's not about name-dropping. It is relationship architecture that others can study and adapt.
- **Record your transformation journey:** When you move from surviving systems to transforming them, your journey contains lessons. Document what worked at each stage and what failed, how you recovered from setbacks, and what you

141 Brown, "Revolutionary Evidence."

would do differently with hindsight. The outcome of this exercise is a road map that new leaders desperately need.

- **Tacit to explicit knowledge:** This is the hardest knowledge to capture because it is the wisdom you know without knowing that you know it. When a Black woman transforms systems for decades, she instinctually makes brilliant moves. She reads rooms instantly and navigates politics effortlessly. However, the reality is that instinct is just automated pattern recognition. The good news is, instinctual insight can be made explicit again by asking exploratory questions of yourself. Questions such as, "Why did I choose that approach?" "What was I responding to?" and "What could I tell someone else facing the same situation?" Asking yourself these questions forces you to externalize your thinking. And that's the goal.

Building for the Next Generation

For us to build for the next generation, we need an understanding of traditional legacy planning, revolutionary legacy planning, the research that informs the difference, the cost of lasting impact, and resource development strategies.

TRADITIONAL LEGACY PLANNING VERSUS REVOLUTIONARY LEGACY PLANNING

Traditional legacy planning asks what you want to leave behind. *Revolutionary legacy* planning asks what the next generation needs to thrive. Constructing an effective revolutionary legacy plan requires a sustainability assessment, vision casting, good culture transformation models, and permission to lead authentically.

Sustainability assessment: Before you can build sustainable power, assess what's actually sustainable.

Questions to ask:

- Does the change you created depend on you personally? If you left tomorrow, would your initiative survive? Or have you built change around yourself instead of into systems?
- Have you documented what you know? Can someone else access your strategic intelligence, or does it live in your head?
- Are you developing successors (not just mentoring people but preparing them to take your seat and hold your power)?
- Have you built collective ownership? Is the work distributed across multiple leaders, or does everything root through you?
- Do you have succession triggers? When will you actively transfer power? What milestone signals transition time?

Vision casting: Your revolutionary legacy planning involves vision casting, a process where you imagine the future we are building toward. The research[142] shows that the next generation is experiencing different challenges, including a more hostile political environment, more sophisticated resistance to equity work, and more backlash against Black women's advancement. At the same time, there are also more tools, more research backing our approaches (such as this book), more Black women in positions of power, and more collective organizing capacity.

Subsequently, effective vision casting requires answering the following question: What does the next generation need from us?

142 Brown, "Revolutionary Evidence."

- **Resilience infrastructure:** Not just the individual grit that makes this sustainable but the collective support systems that sustain leaders through backlash and recovery practices that prevent burnout and encourage community care.
- **Strategic intelligence archives:** Everything we've learned about navigating hostile systems should be documented, accessible, and transferable.
- **Relationship capital networks:** The bridges to power that we've built over decades, connections we can now leverage on behalf of future leaders so they don't have to learn from scratch.
- **Culture transformation models:** Proof that change is possible, such as case studies of successful transformation frameworks that work across different contexts.
- **Permission to lead authentically:** The most valuable aspect that we can pass down is the permission to lead authentically. It's evidence that Revolutionary Pathmakers don't have to sacrifice themselves to succeed. We know that authentic leadership drives results.

RESEARCH VALIDATION

My research reveals shifts in how knowledge needs to transfer. One major shift or trend is that younger Black women leaders are more likely to demand organizational change up front and are less willing to pay dues to systems designed to exclude them. This means they are more comfortable rejecting traditional paths. Simultaneously, they are also more connected to each other. These younger women are building networks across organizations and industries. They are sharing intelligence in real time through digital communities. As a result of these shifts, our transmission model needs to evolve. We need less one-on-one mentoring and more collective knowledge sharing. There must be less waiting for permission and more claiming space to lead.

The next generation won't inherit power the way that we built it. They will demand that it be restructured entirely. Our job is to give them what they need for that fight.

The Cost of Lasting Impact

The cost of lasting impact refers to what sustainability requires. Sustainability costs more than temporary change. It will require us to do the following:

- **Invest time in documentation:** Write down what takes time. Of course, writing things down takes time! In the moment, it feels like inefficiency, but it's the only way your knowledge outlasts you.
- **Develop multiple leaders:** Succession planning means distributing your power while you still hold it. Watching others lead initiatives, you start letting go of control. It is uncomfortable, but it is also necessary.
- **Build collective ownership:** Sustainable change can't center on one person. You must create shared leadership models where multiple people hold pieces of the work. This means that your individual influence feels smaller, but the collective impact grows exponentially.
- **Transfer power before you're ready:** Most leaders wait too long to hand off authority. By the time they're ready, they have created dependency instead of capacity. *Revolutionary*

succession means transferring power while it feels too soon, while you're still valuable and could keep going. And that takes humility and trust.

RESOURCE DEVELOPMENT STRATEGIES

To build revolutionary work that endures, you must develop resources strategically across four essential areas:

- **Financial resources:** The budgets that need to be secured, the funding streams that need to be established, and the financial infrastructures that ensure the work continues.
- **Intellectual resources:** The knowledge that needs to be archived, the training that needs to be developed, and the frameworks that need to be documented.
- **Social capital:** The relationships that need to be transferred, the networks that need to be opened, and the access that needs to be shared.
- **Institutional support:** The policies that need to change, the structures that need to be created, and the systems that need to be redesigned.

You can't pass down what you haven't built. Build with sustainability in mind from the start.

COLLECTIVE LEADERSHIP SESSION MODELS

Traditional succession refers to one person replacing another. Revolutionary succession means collective leadership replacing individual leadership. Instead of finding your replacement, you develop a leadership collective. Through this, multiple people share your former role, distributing power instead of perpetuating concentrated authority. This model prevents the fragility of single points of failure. If one person leaves, the work continues, knowledge stays accessible, and capacity remains strong. This is a model of the future that we're building. Leadership doesn't depend on exceptional individuals. It depends on systems that work for everyone.

KEY TAKEAWAYS

- Your strategic intelligence is too valuable to simply disappear when you leave.
- We need systemic documentation and internal succession planning to preserve revolutionary wisdom.
- Black women, like corporate models, should enable knowledge transfer through formal programs and ensure that their successors have similar access.
- Legacy isn't about what you leave behind. It's about what the next generation needs to thrive.
- Documentation must happen continuously, not at the end.
- Revolutionary succession means restructuring power, not just passing it on. The next generation will redesign it entirely. It's our job to give them the tools for that transformation.

ACTION STEPS

- Start a strategic intelligence journal. Spend fifteen minutes daily documenting one thing that you have learned about navigating your systems or organization.
- Identify three pieces of tacit knowledge you use regularly. Develop explicit frameworks, and explain your thinking so that others can apply your frameworks. Map your relationship ecosystem; e.g., document key connections and how they were developed. Begin introducing potential successors to your network.
- Create your complete legacy documentation system (your strategic intelligence archive), including your decision framework, library relationship map, and transformation journey documentation.

CHAPTER 16

The Revolutionary Investment

Be passionate and move forward with gusto every single hour of every single day until you reach your goal.
AVA DUVERNAY

In this chapter, we will discuss *revolutionary investment*. This is the strategic allocation of energy, time, and resources toward sustainable leadership transformation.

CASE STUDY: WHEN RESEARCH BECOMES MOVEMENT

The little grassroots people can change this world.
WANGARI MAATHAI

Fifteen years after completing my dissertation, I made a decision that surprised many people: I was going to pick up the research again. This time it would be a different study, one tracking how Black women's advancement patterns had evolved. Comparing the 2010 data and 2025 reality, I wanted to see what had changed, what had persisted, what had gotten worse.

I was asked, "You've built a consulting practice, you advise large companies and government agencies, you already have a PhD—why go back to research?"

For me, individual success isn't enough. My 2010 research really quantifies what drives Black women's advancement. Those findings have helped me and my clients. They have helped individual Black women navigate corporate systems more strategically.

But here's what kept me up at night: I was still teaching navigation, still helping people succeed within systems designed to resist them. I was still focused on individual advancement rather than collective transformation.

My 2025 research asked different questions, not just "How do women advance?" but "What would advancement systems look like if designed from equity from the start?" Not just "What strategies work?" but "What structural changes eliminated the need for these strategies?" Not just "How do individuals succeed?" but "How do we create collective transformation?"

These shifts reflect something bigger happening: Black women I work with aren't just trying to climb ladders anymore. They're building different structures entirely. Starting businesses, creating platforms, and designing systems that center equity and humanity instead of adding it later. My work needed to match this evolution.

So I designed an ecosystem, not just a book. Research findings become accessible frameworks. This book reaches individual leaders. The podcast builds community speaking engagements and creates organizational entry points. Digital tools extend the work beyond my direct contact.

I invested in some cohorts for small businesses, one being Goldman Sachs supporting a thousand small businesses. I did this not because my consultancy was failing but because revolutionary work requires infrastructure. I needed to understand business systems well enough to build sustainable transformation, not just inspiring ideas.

You see, I am planning for success before I need it. I am creating frameworks others can use and training practitioners who will take this work further. At the same time, I am designing tools that will outlive me. This is because fifteen years have taught me that individual advancement creates ripples, while collective transformation creates waves.

Revolutionary work means building systems that continue after you're gone. The work ahead isn't about me succeeding; it's about creating conditions where the next generation doesn't have to navigate the same barriers. A future in which the frameworks I'm building become foundations others build on. That's revolutionary work. Not climbing higher, but creating different architecture entirely.

POWER ACTIVATION PROMPT

What price have you paid for leadership? What recovery strategies keep you whole while driving change? Where are you investing energy that depletes without advancing you?

Naming the Hidden Costs

Black women have always paid double for leadership: the work itself and the work of doing it while navigating hostile systems. Whether you are inside an organization or own your business, these systems are applicable to you.

Traditional leadership literature talks about work-life balance, as though everyone starts at the same place. Revolutionary leadership recognizes that Black women are doing multiple jobs simultaneously: representation work, navigation work, and the actual work. As a result, there are three cost factors that Black women manage simultaneously:

- **Performativity tax:** This is the cost of having every action scrutinized differently, every mistake magnified, and every success attributed to luck or affirmative action rather than competence. This isn't paranoia. It's documented reality that requires extra energy and effort.
- **Representation weight:** You are never just yourself. You are representing Black women as a category. Your stumbling becomes evidence about the group. As a result, your success must be managed carefully so that you don't trigger backlash. The cognitive load is constant and exhausting.

- **Navigation energy:** This is the cost related to code-switching, culture translation, reading rooms for safety, managing others' discomfort with your presence, and deciding which battles matter. This is invisible labor that happens with every single interaction.

The research shows us that the cost hasn't decreased, despite organizational and societal claims of progress.[143] It has just become more visible as companies and society realize that diverse teams outperform even though Black women still carry a disproportionate burden.

The Impact Assessment Framework

To understand the degree of hidden costs each of us bears, we must analyze every impact and its cost. That is the purpose of the Impact Assessment Framework. In this analysis, we evaluate the following:

- **Beyond burnout language:** Companies counter burnout with corporate wellness programs with meditation apps and mental health days that soothe the individual but ignore the structural problems. The literature, frameworks, and analysis around burnout miss what's happening when you're simultaneously transforming systems and surviving them. It is necessary to have different tools to assess the real impact. Enter the Impact Assessment Framework.

THE REVOLUTIONARY IMPACT INVENTORY

- **Physical impact measures:** The sleep disruption patterns aren't just insomnia but hypervigilance. The related health

143 Brown, "Revolutionary Evidence."

changes your doctor can't quite explain are connected to work. One sure indicator of energy depletion is that days off don't fix it.

- **Mental impact measures:** Decision fatigue comes from constant navigation. It isn't that you are just tired; it is mental depletion from making hundreds of micro-decisions about code-switching, safety, and strategy. Code-switching carries with it the cognitive load of the dual consciousness, where you see both what's happening and what it means. Strategic thinking capacity is diminished as the dual consciousness takes over.
- **Emotional impact measures:** The emotional labor intensity that goes unmeasured and uncompensated. Managing others' feelings about your presence, your success, and your boundaries, the way excessive work demands strain your relationships and render you unavailable to or irritable with the people you love. Joy depletion indicators, a subset of emotional impact measures, appear when things that used to refuel you feel more like obligations. For example, I love spending time with my children, but sometimes I'm so busy and drained that it feels like a chore to spend time with them. I want to do fun things as a family, but when I'm emotionally depleted, all I want to do is sit at home and do nothing.
- **Professional impact measures:** This is the time spent on activities that, as my research and that of others show, doesn't advance careers.[144] This includes the 60/10 problem discussed in chapter 14, whereby 60 percent of the time you spend on activities often contributes to only 10 percent of your goals.

144 Brown, "Revolutionary Evidence."

- **Structural theft:** All the above may not necessarily constitute burnout but what I call structural theft. If you combine an understanding of burnout with the impacts outlined previously, you may come to realize that these are what the structures rob you of. In reality, organizations and systems are extracting value while blocking your advancement or progress.
- **Investment calculation:** When you combine this understanding of what lies beyond the burnout language with the insights from your personalized Revolutionary Impact Inventory, you can track which activities produce returns versus which just produce costs.

Again, drawing from my own personal experience, this time from my consultancy practice, I have found that most women I work with are shocked when they complete this inventory. These women are investing heavily in activities that organizations and systems might praise, but their careers aren't being rewarded for the same.

Revolutionary Recovery Strategies

If you carry out your own impact assessment using the aforementioned framework, you may discover that you need restoration. Here are several revolutionary recovery strategies that may help you do just that:

- **Historical:** Black women have pioneered strategic restoration for generations in the different communities they are a part of. Church mothers rested on purpose. Community organizers built support circles or sister circles for refueling. Professionals protected Sunday dinners and Friday night rituals. They have long understood something that has only recently been acknowledged in the working world: the concept of wellness.

Black women realized that, as the saying goes, "you can't pour from an empty cup." Refueling isn't selfish; it's strategic.

- **Radical self-care as a revolutionary practice:** It's not bubble baths and face masks. Radical self-awareness as a revolutionary practice is strategic resource management that protects your capacity to lead, recognizing that preservation of the self enables the transformation of systems. Typically, we are advised to set boundaries. But revolutionary recovery requires designing systems where sustainable choices become easier than destructive ones.
- **Boundary architecture:** It isn't about saying no to everything but building structures where yes serves as advancement, and no protects your capacity. For example, when I built my consulting practice, I didn't just reduce the hours I worked; I redesigned how I worked. I set client boundaries about after-hours communication. My project selection criteria were based on the advancement of things that worked for me, my intellectual curiosity, and my excitement about the work, not just the revenue. There were people I could have taken on as clients and made a lot of money, but I didn't like them or the work I would be doing, so I declined.
- **Strategic energy:** We know the research shows that most Black women spend a disproportionate amount of time on low-impact activities.[145] [146] Strategic energy allocation means the return matches the investment. Again, we must consider the 60/10 problem discussed in chapter 14.

145 Jones, "Quantitative Study."

146 Brown, "Revolutionary Evidence."

THREE RECOVERY TIERS

Your recovery is unique, as the degree and level of it depend largely on the extent of depletion you have endured. However, here are some rough guidelines to help you get started:

- **Daily recovery practices:** This may involve turning off your phone and not answering emails when the workday is done. If you are an entrepreneur or work from home, as I do, I suggest you close your office door at a particular time and Ieave your devices, iPad, laptop, and work phone in your office. Deliberately engage in joy protection practices, such as picking up your kids after school and learning about what their school day was like. This may mean putting those things into your schedule to protect that time for pickup and drop off.
- **Weekly restoration systems:** This could include regular therapy sessions and similar efforts. This isn't crisis management, it's strategic processing for navigating your professional life.
- **Quarterly renewal process:** Give a full assessment of your energy in terms of ROI. Analyze what's working, what's depleting you without advancement, and where you are investing a lot of time with little return. This includes:
- **Relationship evaluation:** Self-evaluate whether your connections are refueling you or extracting from you.
- **Aspiration realignment:** Determine if your goals are still yours, or if they have become what others expect.
- **Community recovery model:** Black women have always known that isolation depletes and community restores. Church circles for authentic sharing, sister circles where you can show up with what you are holding, and professional

networks where you can be strategic without apology are not just spaces for venting. They are sanctuaries for strategically refueling systems.

Designing Support Systems for Sustainability

SUPPORT ARCHITECTURE

Designing and building support systems that are sustainable doesn't happen by accident. Most support advice assumes privilege. Support design recognizes that you're building with less and sometimes under pressure and therefore need support architectures that are intentionally designed to hold when pressure intensifies. There are four essential system components:

1. PROFESSIONAL SUPPORT NETWORK

These are specified roles filled by specific people, and not just generic networking. Within these professional support networks, you can find these specific people:

- **Individual visibility advocates:** People inside the organization or industry who make your contributions visible to decision-makers. As discussed, research shows that this matters statistically. But most Black women under-source this critical support.
- **Strategic counsel:** People who help you navigate the system's politics without exhausting yourself. They can decode the hidden rules, and they understand unstated expectations.

- **Skill development partners:** Relationships focused on capacity building, not just emotional support.
- **Advancement intelligence sources:** People who tell you about opportunities before they are public and who sponsor the assignments that matter.

2. EMOTIONAL SUPPORT INFRASTRUCTURE

- **Therapist:** A regular session with someone who understands your professional ambition, racial pressures, and gender navigation.
- **Sister circle:** Black women who get it without explanation, in a space where you can be strategic, ambitious, exhausted, angry, and even joyful without performing any particular version of blackness.
- **Mentor/coach relationships:** People who are ahead of you and will remind you of what this stage costs and can normalize your experience while helping you to navigate forward.
- **Safe processing spaces:** Relationships in which you can say the things that are unsayable and rest without performing rest.

3. PRACTICAL SUPPORT SYSTEMS

- **Childcare backup plans:** So your work doesn't collapse when one system fails.
- **Household delegation:** Traditionally, women have been expected to keep house. Figure out what genuinely requires you versus what you're doing.

- **Time-protection mechanisms:** Systems that guard your strategic work time from constant interruption.
- **Energy conservation tools:** Automate decisions that don't matter so you have capacity for the ones that do.

4. RESTORATION SUPPORT

- **Regular self-care practices:** Build these into your routine and use them. They are not saved for crisis.
- **Quarterly renewal processes:** Schedule check-ins before exhaustion forces them.
- **Annual strategic reassessment:** A full evaluation of your investments, returns, and aspirations.
- **Joy preservation rituals:** Protect your time for the things that refuel you.

THE SUSTAINABILITY TEST

This is a simple test where you ask yourself, *Can this system survive the pressure?*

When you think about creating or designing your support system for sustainability, you really want to test it.

Another question that you must ask yourself is, *Does it require that I sacrifice again to maintain it?*

The reality is that unsustainable support needs constant attention. Sustainable support runs in the background, and it catches you before a crisis.

KEY TAKEAWAYS

- Leadership costs Black women triple.
- Recovery is strategic, not selfish.
- Support needs architecture, not accidents.
- Investment requires honest calculation.
- Sustainably is tested under pressure.

ACTION STEPS

- Complete the Revolutionary Impact Inventory; be honest about the cost, and calculate energy out and investment in.
- Choose one recovery system, whether daily, weekly, or quarterly. Design it, implement it, and protect it for thirty days and see what happens.
- Audit your support architecture: Map what exists across all four components, identify what's missing, and start building, one gap at a time.
- Reassess energy ROI quarterly, and adjust investments based on research-backed advancement drivers. Protect your capacity while pursuing your aspiration, and build recovery into structures, not crisis response.

CHAPTER 17

The Revolutionary Work Ahead

The way to right wrongs is to turn the light of truth upon them.
IDA B. WELLS

In this chapter, we will close our in-depth exposition of revolutionary leadership by exploring the work that still lies before us. Without a doubt, the work ahead involves building sustainable transformation through strategic visioning.

CASE STUDY: MARION STOKES

Instead of looking at the past, I put myself ahead twenty years and try to look at what I need to do now in order to get there then.
DIANA ROSS

Marion Marguerite Stokes (née Butler) remains a unique Revolutionary Pathmaker, especially when it comes to her service and dedication for the sake of future generations. Born in 1929 in

Pennsylvania, she worked for twenty years as a librarian at the Free Library of Philadelphia. During that time, she became a civil rights activist.[147]

Following a prominent hostage situation in 1979, the Iran hostage crisis, Stokes noticed some inconsistencies in the reports. She believed there was a cover-up underway. This led to her recording news broadcasts to guard the truth for posterity.[148]

"She had eight televisions and recorders stationed throughout the family homes that were on twenty-four hours a day … Stokes bought and labeled tapes and then stored her work. She often woke up early to record or came home during the day to check on her work. She cut dinners short to get home to change tapes. When she became too old to keep up with her work, Stokes hired an assistant and trained him to run the tapes for her."[149]

From the day she started recording to the day she died, Stokes never stopped. Stokes, labeled by some as "ahead of her time," had recorded over seventy thousand tapes of footage and fifty thousand books. Her recordings included news about man walking on the moon, JFK's assassination, and the Challenger explosion.[150] *Documentary director Matt Wolf, who produced a documentary about Stokes's life's work, realized why she had kept so much information. Wolf stated, "History takes on*

147 Euell A. Dixon, "Marion Marguerite Butler Stokes (1929–2012)," *BlackPast.org*, February 9, 2020, https://blackpast.org/african-american-history/marion-marguerite-butler-stokes-1929-2012.

148 Ibid.

149 Ibid.

150 Ammar Kalia, "'Ahead of Her Time': The Woman Who Recorded the News for 30 Years," *The Guardian*, October 4, 2019, https://www.theguardian.com/film/2019/oct/04/giant-cookies-and-911-the-woman-who-recorded-the-news-24-hours-a-day.

greater meaning as time passes, and Marion was so invested in knowledge and truth—it's just that she didn't know what would have meaning or truth in the future, so she had to record it all."[151]

Upon Stoke's passing, her only child donated her archive to the Internet Archive, a resource that allows anyone, anywhere, to access these records and more.[152]

This Revolutionary Pathmaker's radical dedication to protect the truth for future generations is exactly what revolutionary leadership is all about. Stokes didn't just recognize that something was important. She built the systems to preserve it. This was guerrilla archiving before we even had the language for it. And, though people only realized it once she passed away and her archives were donated for all the world to benefit from, this was revolutionary leadership.

POWER ACTIVATION PROMPT

What revolutionary work are you building toward? What possibilities will you create for those who follow? How will your leadership extend beyond your lifetime?

151 Ibid.

152 Queen Muse, "Librarian Recorded 800,000 Hours of News Over 35 Years, Leaves Behind Massive Archive," *NBC News*, December 7, 2013, https://www.nbcnews.com/news/us-news/librarian-recorded-800-000-hours-news-over-35-years-leaves-flna2d11709280.

From Surviving Systems to Redesigning Them

Black women have always led with vision. This was not despite constraints but because of them. When traditional paths were blocked, we created new ones. This included starting schools when excluded from existing institutions, building businesses when employment was denied, and shifting the direction and priorities of organizations when leadership was gatekept. But none of the nature of that visionary work has evolved across eras. Therefore, there must be a shift from access to representation and then on to transformation.

Research Validation

Across the 2010[153] and 2025[154] studies, the most significant evolution was not only where Black women worked but how they redefined participation in the systems themselves. In the earlier research, much of the women's labor centered on learning to navigate existing structures—sustaining visibility, building access, and creating stability inside environments that were not designed with Black women in mind. By 2025, many Black women were no longer investing their energy in adapting to those structures alone. They were making strategic decisions about when to remain inside them, when to reshape them, and when to build entirely new spaces of leadership, ownership, and care.

The research shows that this shift is not simply entrepreneurial or occupational; it is philosophical. Black women are treating institutions as sites of conditional engagement rather than automatic loyalty.

153 Jones, "Quantitative Study."

154 Brown, "Revolutionary Evidence."

They are leveraging experience and resources gained inside organizations to fuel community work, entrepreneurial ecosystems, and the collaborative networks beyond them. Participation has become intentional, time bound, and purpose driven. The question is no longer "How do we succeed within the system?" but "Does this system align with the futures we are trying to build?"

The work ahead, then, is not only about preparing Black women to survive demanding structures—it is about equipping them with frameworks for discernment, collective strategy, and world-building so that leadership becomes not a test of endurance but a pathway to transformation.

The Opportunity Creation Framework

Traditional career advice teaches opportunity recognition. That means scanning job boards, networking strategically, and positioning yourself for openings. Revolutionary leadership requires opportunity creation. This means creating something and building possibilities that didn't exist before. The following is the CREATE Methodology for creating those opportunities.

THE CREATE METHODOLOGY

- **C**larify the gap: Identify what doesn't exist but should—not just for you, but for people who follow you or that you lead. You must manage the gap recognition. Where research exists but isn't accessible, where possible, make it accessible.
- **R**esearch what's worked elsewhere: Study how others have created similar opportunities. What worked, what failed, and what you can adapt.

- Enlist collective intelligence: Black women's visionary traditions have always been collective—build those sister circles, professional networks, and community wisdom.
- Architect multiple pathways: Don't assume that there's one right route. Design several paths with the same destination.
- Test and iterate quickly: Don't just wait for your perfect launch and learn.
- Extend beyond yourself: This is a revolutionary part. Create opportunities that multiply and serve others, not just you. This means frameworks that others can adapt, tools for practitioners to use with their clients, and models that work in multiple contexts. Note: If this helps only you, it's not revolutionary. It's just personal success.

The ecosystem multiplies impact. For example, when one person reads this book and shares the framework with their team, organizations implement changes, and multiple Black women benefit. When Black women benefit, everyone benefits.

It is worth noting that this is about building platforms and not climbing ladders. Through my research analysis, I noted that women are increasingly thinking this way. It's no longer just about how you get promoted but about how the platform you build can advance multiple people.[155] It's not just how you succeed but how the structure you create redistributes opportunity. This shift from individual to collective represents a revolutionary evolution.

155 Brown, "Revolutionary Evidence."

Revolutionary Innovation Methodology

We must move from idea to implementation and then to impact. Vision without method creates chaos. For effective planning, you need structure.

THE INNOVATE PLANNING PROCESS

- **I**dentify transformation targets: What specifically needs to change? It cannot be everything, because that's overwhelming, so pick targets strategically. Each target should serve a larger transformation goal while remaining concrete.
- **N**avigate constraints strategically: Plan for how you will navigate real limitations, such as time, money, energy, and access. Then design around them creatively. Carry out your tasks one piece at a time. Use digital tools that allow you to scale without requiring your constant presence. You need to be able to answer how you get information and generate revenue without having to strategically be with everyone every single time there is an engagement.
- **N**urture prototype solutions: Test ideas at a small scale. Before scaling, learn what works without massive investment.
- **O**rganize coalition support: Revolutionary work requires community. Identify who needs to support this and build those relationships intentionally. Each relationship gets strategic attention, which we validate with evidence.
- **V**alidate with evidence: Don't assume. Test and measure what's working and what's not. Track which frameworks resonate, which tools get used, and which content creates transformation versus which just get consumed. Adjust based on the

evidence, not assumptions about what should work or what you want to work.

- Adjust based on feedback: Innovation requires continuous refinement, so build feedback loops into the design. Include monthly check-ins with some early users, quarterly content adjustments, and annual strategic reassessment. It is vital to stay responsive without being reactive.
- Transfer to others: This is the revolutionary part. You must create frameworks that others can use independently. The goal is that the work continues without you.
- Evaluate impact continuously: Continuously measure revolutionary progress and not just the traditional matrix.

INNOVATION CATEGORIES

Most organizations focus on product innovation. Revolutionary work requires a paradigm of innovation—not just new tools but new ways of understanding the problems themselves.

You may wonder where you can begin maximizing innovation, so consider the following:

- Products: New products and product innovation.
- Process: New methodologies, including frameworks, road maps, and templates.
- Platform: New infrastructure; that is, an ecosystem approach, such as partnering and engaging with other practitioners.
- Paradigm: New ways of thinking; revolutionary work requires paradigm innovation.

RESEARCH

My 2010 research[156] revealed advancement drivers. Innovation planning applies those insights systematically. My 2025 research[157] informs the next innovation cycle. There has been an evolution, particularly in terms of advancement patterns. There are also shifts in what drives success. Recognizing this positions me for an ongoing innovation and frameworks update with current data. Simultaneously, we still have the historical grounding in current relevance and continuous evolution rather than a onetime publication.

Measuring Revolutionary Progress

Accurately measuring revolutionary progress requires considering moving beyond just representation and retention rates. Diversity, training, hours of activity, employee satisfaction scores, perception, and oftentimes, retention rates matter—in part because they are stable. But while they matter, they don't measure revolutionary change. When it comes to representation, the traditional organization matrix simply counts women in leadership. But measuring revolutionary transformation requires moving beyond simple numbers.

Measuring revolutionary progress requires new indicators.

REVOLUTIONARY PROGRESS INDICATORS

POWER DISTRIBUTION CHANGES

Who makes decisions now? Is this different from before? It's not about who sits in meetings, but who has actual authority. Tracking budget control, hiring authority, strategic direction setting, and policy

156 Jones, "Quantitative Study."

157 Brown, "Revolutionary Evidence."

creation reveal the real power. If Black women are in leadership, but white men still make all the decisions, that's representation without transformation.

SYSTEM DESIGN DEPTH

Consider surface changes versus structural transformation. Surface changes include diversity statements, bias training, and employee resource groups. Structural changes rebuild the pipeline through a redesign of evaluation criteria and promotion policies. It's vital to measure how deep the changes go. Understand whether they are policies, practices, systems, or culture.

COLLECTIVE ADVANCEMENT

Revolutionary change is all about group mobility, not individual success. The traditional matrix celebrates tokens, such as when one Black woman reaches the executive level. If only exceptional individuals succeed, then the system hasn't changed. The revolutionary matrix tracks the collective movement of Black women as a group. Advancement means pathways are being created for multiple people.

SUSTAINABILITY UNDER PRESSURE

Leadership changes, budgets get cut, and then comes resistance. Sometimes, champions leave. So, the test of your transformation work is: Does your work survive? Does the work continue even if the economy tightens, and there is backlash against equity commitments? Revolutionary change is built to last through opposition.

AMPLIFICATION RESEARCH

Quantify how many people use your frameworks and how far beyond you your impact extends. If transformation only happens where you're personally present, it's not a movement; it's individual influence. Revolutionary work multiplies your frameworks and gets used by people you'll never meet. Your tools spread beyond your direct network. Your impact extends past your lifetime.

THE PROGRESS DASHBOARD

Track transformation across multiple dimensions simultaneously. Individual advancement, Black women's promotion rates, and collective mobility are key dimensions you can track for group advancement patterns.

System changes are policy and practice shifts. Power redistribution of decision authority changes cultural transformation, belonging, and inclusion measures. Sustainability indicators measure if the change persists over time. No single matrix captures revolutionary progress. You need a comprehensive dashboard to look at the changes in their entirety.

WHY MEASURING MATTERS

Evidence drives continued investment. Organizations fund what gets measured. Funders support what shows results. Leaders protect what demonstrates value. If you can't prove transformation is happening, resources disappear when the pressure increases. Measurement isn't bureaucracy; it's the protection of revolutionary work.

Amplification Strategies

Going beyond your own success is an effort in multiplication or amplification. Revolutionary work doesn't end with you; it begins with you, and it extends indefinitely. One way to think about strategy is through the AMPLIFY Framework.

THE AMPLIFY FRAMEWORK

- **A**rticulate transferable frameworks:
  Create tools others can use without you. Use stories. Share processes, adaptable frameworks, and clear methodologies.

- **M**entor the next generation:
  Invest in people who take work further. Move beyond advice to offer actual skill transfer frameworks, training, and practical support.

- **P**ublish accessible insights:
  Make knowledge available beyond academic circles. Research lives in dissertations that nobody reads. Revolutionary work translates those findings into formats.

- **L**everage multiple platforms:
  Don't rely on a single channel; build an ecosystem that reinforces itself.

- **I**nvite collaboration:
  Revolutionary work requires collective efforts, so create entry points for others to contribute. Open-source some tools, create a practitioner community, build collaborative networks, and make space for others to extend the work.

- **F**und infrastructure:
  Revolutionary work needs sustainable financial foundations. Infrastructure needs revenue, and sustainability demands financial planning. Move from passion for the work to practical business foundations that enable the work to continue.

- **Y**ield leadership to others:

> Plan for your exit from the beginning. Train people to lead without you. Create systems that run independently; build structures that outlive you. If your work dies when you leave, it wasn't revolutionary. It was personal influence. This is the revolutionary part: preparing for continued challenges.

History tells us to expect resistance to our revolutionary work. It is important to be prepared for this resistance and to be able to respond in ways that will allow the work to continue.

ANTICIPATED RESISTANCE PATTERNS

Pushback from external systems and internal doubt is predictable. The pushback cycle has three phases:

Phase one: Celebration. Initial wins get praised—for example, "Our first Black woman executive." Many of us have heard or experienced organizations celebrating without changing.

Phase two: Redirection. Progress triggers resistance, the feeling that we've done enough of this type of diversity, inclusion, and belonging work. Then resources get redirected and commitments soften.

Phase three: Regulation. Laws and policies are developed that attempt to restrict progress. DEI work gets banned.

BUILDING RESILIENCE INTO REVOLUTIONARY WORK

In phase three, equity initiatives face legal challenges. We must prepare accordingly by building resistance into our revolutionary work.

COALITION STRATEGIES FOR WEATHERING OPPOSITION

Don't work alone. You must build networks of support during opposition waves: sister circles that hold you, professional alliances that back you, a community infrastructure that sustains you.

WHEN THE WORK REQUIRES LONG-TERM COMMITMENT

Building resistance is a long-term commitment. Revolutionary work requires decades, not months. This isn't a sprint; it's a marathon requiring sustained commitment through multiple resistance cycles. Prepare for the long game.

PROTECTING GAINS WHILE PUSHING FORWARD

Lock in changes structurally: Codify policies, and institutionalize practices. Accountability built on surface changes gets reversed easily. Structural changes persist through opposition.

The work continues because the alternative is unacceptable. The next generation deserves better. Transformation is possible even when it's difficult. And revolutionary work isn't optional; it's necessary.

Organizations Leading Revolutionary Change

Fortunately, we have a host of examples and common success patterns that can assist us in realizing revolutionary change.

EXAMPLES

As I write this, there are a lot of promising initiatives underway. Some organizations are moving beyond performative behaviors to a structural transformation that better protects and positively impacts the bottom line.

A few companies are designing evaluation systems that value diverse leadership styles, creating advancement pathways that don't require code-switching, and building accountability for equity outcomes at the highest levels in their organizations. This is ongoing and still in the early days.

While it has been fragile, movement is happening in the nonprofit sector. Organizations are incorporating participatory governance, redistributing decision-making power, and redesigning leadership cultures for collective authority. Results are still emerging because it's a long journey, but the approach is promising.

Some universities are questioning traditional hierarchies by creating alternative pathways to promotion that value community knowledge alongside research knowledge. Some companies, particularly those with new founders and founders of color, are building equity into their product designs from the start, creating diverse teams with actual authority and measuring inclusion beyond representation.

COMMON SUCCESS PATTERNS

Organizations that succeed share some characteristics. Leadership commits to transformation, not just optics. Resources are assigned to structural change, not just training. Accountability is built into operations, not just initiative and measurement tracking. There is power distribution, not just representation.

KEY TAKEAWAYS

- The work shifts from navigation to redesign.
- Opportunity creation requires methodology.
- The traditional matrix misses revolutionary progress.

- Amplification extends impact.
- Resistance is predictable and manageable.

ACTION STEPS

- Identify one opportunity you can create. Think about what doesn't exist but should. What gap can you fill that serves multiple people, not just you?
- Apply the CREATE Methodology to one possibility. Work through all six steps, and clarify the gap. Research approaches that offer collective intelligence. Test quickly, and extend beyond yourself.
- Begin innovative planning for one transformation project. Identify targets, navigate constraints, nurture prototypes, etc. Start small, but think systematically about how to scale your work.
- Design one amplification strategy that extends your impact beyond your direct contact. Create frameworks that others can use. Train other people on how to use them. Build capacity and community. Measure your reach beyond yourself.

CONCLUSION

Revolution Realized

At the very beginning, in chapter 1, I introduced to you the concept of Revolutionary Pathmakers. Together, we explored stories and case studies of many phenomenal women. By now, I hope we can agree that these models of excellence are not only numerous but also diverse in their achievements. Each contributes toward their communities, and humanity, in remarkable ways.

Throughout the book, we looked at

- survival and transformation,
- the linkage between individual and systemic change,
- research and lived experience,
- hope and possibility while acknowledging challenges,
- the centering of Black women's agency and power,
- sustainability and long-term impact, and
- the uniqueness of Black women's position as both subjects and change agents.

I encourage you to use this book as a reference and guide. *Revolutionary Leadership* is deliberately dense so that I leave you no gaps in knowledge that impede your success. My goal is for you to have everything you need to win, wherever you are.

As we close, I hope you remain confident in this:

- All the successful efforts that you make as a Black woman are likely validated by historical presence and research. Go forward confidently and without second-guessing yourself.
- *Yes, you can have it all!* But you must be strategic in acquiring that happy home and successful career. It takes time, innovation, and effort, but I promise you, it's possible.
- You can give yourself permission to let go of what didn't serve you and reach toward what will.
- The communities (sister groups, networking groups, and wherever else you find yourself) are more valuable than hustle culture will have us believe. Nurturing these connections is an exercise of great wisdom, especially in the current socioeconomic climate.

Let this book be a constant reminder that you are seen and that your contribution to your community and the world is appreciated, important, and desperately needed.

Now, let's continue this legacy of revolutionary leadership.

TO THOSE WHO SHOW UP

This is for the people who get it. The ones who hold space without trying to fix everything. Who listen when we need to be heard and stand back when we need to lead.

You see us. Not the versions of us the world expects but who we actually are. You make room for our fullness. Our joy. Our rage. Our quiet moments and our loud ones.

You celebrate us when we win and don't shrink when we outgrow old spaces. You understand that loving a Black woman means protecting her peace, not her fragility. Because we are not fragile. We're just tired of fighting alone.

Thank you for choosing partnership over performance. For showing up consistently, not perfectly. For creating the kind of safety that lets us put down our armor and just breathe and laugh.

Thank you for the soul link. The rare connection where words aren't always needed, where you feel before we speak. Where our spirits recognize each other in a way that goes deeper than logic or timing. You know when to hold us close and when to give us space. That's not luck. That's attunement.

And yes, thank you for the great sex. The kind that's about connection, not just bodies. Where we feel desired and safe at the same time. Where pleasure isn't transactional. Where you care as much about our satisfaction as your own. That matters more than people admit.

You prove that love doesn't have to be loud to be real. That support doesn't require a spotlight. That being seen is sometimes the most radical gift you can give.

This work exists because of the people who love Black women well. Who know our magic isn't something to consume but something to protect. Who understand that when we thrive, everyone around us does too.

We see you. And we're grateful.

ACKNOWLEDGMENTS

Revolutionary Leadership is more than the result of thirty years as a scholar-practitioner. It is my "soul work," work that would not exist if it were not for the multitudes of people who have helped me in my personal life, academic journey, and professional career, and I offer them my deepest gratitude for directly and indirectly contributing to the realization and development of this book.

I would like to thank my husband, Sherman Lee Brown Jr. Sherman, you have been my unwavering partner, provider, and anchor. Your belief in me, whether I was chasing a new degree, launching a bold vision, or navigating the quiet work of healing, has been constant and true. There is not a dream, pivot, or possibility that I pursued that you did not support without hesitation. You are perfect for me. Your love and steadiness have been a foundation for our life, our family, and the work I have been called to do. This journey is ours, and this book carries your imprint too. Revolutionary leadership is never done in isolation. Much of my success is possible because I knew you were cheering me on.

My gratitude also goes to Dr. Charlene Sinclair, who embodied revolutionary leadership for me in ways that made it feel not only attainable but something I, too, could empower in others. Your passion for social transformation at the intersection of race, gender, economics, and democracy continues to inspire me. Charlene, you are one of the most brilliant and courageous women I know. Your relentless commitment to justice is truly inspiring. Not only are you my dear friend, but you are also the sister I didn't know I needed until I met you, and my number one coconspirator. Your presence challenges and uplifts everyone around you. I am grateful to you for the wisdom you freely share, your powerful example of humanity, and the generosity of your sisterhood. Your life and leadership serve as a reminder that transformation is possible when we lead with integrity, purpose, and deep love. The privilege to walk alongside you and witness what it means to lead from the soul is priceless.

My first and lifelong best friends: Tanya Young Rucker and Catrina Barker Fowler. You were my earliest mirrors, truth-tellers, and cheerleaders. Your unwavering presence has been a quiet force behind every bold step I have taken. In a world that often asks women to compete, you taught me the sacred power of sisterhood: of showing up, holding space, and lifting one another higher. This book is rooted in the kind of love, laughter, and loyalty we have shared for decades. Thank you for shaping the woman and leader that I have become.

To my sisters, Keish Mitchell and Gail Mitchell Jackson, who are part of every story I carry.

My children: Olivia, Charles, Saige, and Sherman III—thank you. This is my legacy, which you have inspired in me. My daughters, Olivia and Saige—you are my very own Revolutionary Pathmakers. I knew it the moment I saw each of you take your first breath. Your power fuels mine.

To the great host of Revolutionary Pathmakers whom I was privileged enough to be raised, nurtured, or taught by, and to those I only get to read about in books, thank you. Your lessons continue to inspire me to this day.

Lastly, I am grateful to you, dear reader. I offer this gift of wisdom and insights from my lived experience, a great host of Revolutionary Pathmakers, and rigorous research.

Thank you.

ABOUT THE AUTHOR

Dr. Kerry Mitchell Brown fixes the dysfunction most consultants won't name.

As CEO of kmb Consultancy, she works with Fortune 100 companies, government agencies, and institutions stuck in cycles of structural breakdown. Her clients don't hire her for workshops. They hire her because their executive teams are fractured, their systems protect the wrong behaviors, and traditional consulting hasn't worked.

Dr. Brown spent a decade in corporate, government, and nonprofit leadership, another decade in higher education, and nearly another decade running her own consulting practice. She knows how decisions get made in government agencies. She understands procurement rules, civil service constraints, and the institutional resistance that kills most transformation efforts before they start. That combination makes her irreplaceable to clients who are navigating complex bureaucracies.

Her approach is direct. She doesn't facilitate conversations about equity. She redesigns systems so they function for everyone who works in them. She strengthens boards and executive teams by addressing the power dynamics and cultural patterns that create dysfunction in the first place.

Dr. Brown also works one-on-one with Black women leaders who are done performing and are ready to lead from a position of power. Her coaching clients aren't looking for affirmations. They're building strategies to advance in environments that weren't designed for them. They want someone who understands the game and can help them play it without losing themselves.

Before founding kmb Consultancy, Dr. Brown held senior leadership roles across private, nonprofit, and government sectors. She's led transformation work for over fifty organizations and partnered directly with nearly 250 leaders. Her research and insights have been featured in *Forbes*, *Bloomberg*, *Black Enterprise*, and *Business Insider*.

She holds a PhD in organizations and management, where her research focused on quantifying strategic advancement for Black women leaders. She also holds an MBA and a BSBA in Finance and is certified in Gestalt Organization and Systems Development.

Dr. Brown hosts the *Revolutionary Leadership: Where Black Women's Stories Become Tomorrow's Blueprints* podcast, which treats lived experience as data and uses it to build new models for leadership.

Originally from Omaha, Nebraska, Dr. Brown now lives between Chicago and Orlando with her husband, Sherman, and their twins, Saige and Sherman III. She also enjoys time with her adult children, Olivia and Charles. When not working, she cooks, travels, and reads.

To work with Dr. Brown or to bring her into your organization, visit https://kerrymitchellbrown.com.

www.ingramcontent.com/pod-product-compliance
Lightning Source LLC
LaVergne TN
LVHW041604220426
836989LV00004B/14
9798897010615